[UN] EMBARRASSED
OF JESUS

TRAVIS JOHNSON

CHARISMA
HOUSE

It's been said that courage is the testing point of every virtue. In *(Un)Embarrassed of Jesus*, Pastor Johnson delivers a desperately needed, biblically grounded altar call for American Christians, challenging them to find the courage to follow Jesus loudly and proudly—even as the culture around them grows increasingly hostile to the faith that founded this nation. It's time for believers to take a stand on the side of Christ, come what may. And Pastor Johnson's book provides us with the encouragement and correction and a shot in the arm of spiritual boldness to do just that.

—WILLIAM WOLFE
EXECUTIVE DIRECTOR, CENTER FOR BAPTIST LEADERSHIP

My good friend Pastor Travis Johnson challenges us to boldly believe and courageously follow Jesus in a culture that is collapsing and a church that is so often sinfully silent. My prayer is that many will read this outstanding book and commit to never being ashamed of our wonderful Savior.

—JACK GRAHAM
LEAD PASTOR, PRESTONWOOD BAPTIST CHURCH

Travis is a pastor who "knows what time it is," as we say in our business. He knows the time for cowardly and complacent Christianity is over, for there never was any such thing. This is not a contemplative exercise but a mission field. And Travis is on mission.

—STEVE DEACE
BEST-SELLING AUTHOR; HOST, *STEVE DEACE SHOW*

Pastor Travis is a clear voice for this generation, shattering the myth of casual Christianity. With unwavering courage and conviction, he calls people to embrace the truth and speak it without reservation. He is a mentor to many, including myself. Reading this book will challenge you to go live boldly for Christ.

—BARRY MOORE
MEMBER OF CONGRESS

Pastor Travis Johnson is a man of courage and conviction. What I admire most is that he's an even better man behind the scenes than he is in public. In a generation desperate for authentic leaders, Travis models humility, integrity, and faithfulness.

(Un)Embarrassed of Jesus is more than a title; it's a call to the church in this hour. His voice carries a needed challenge to believers: to stand boldly, live authentically, and be unashamed of Christ. This book will stir courage in your heart and clarity in your walk with Jesus.

—LANDON SCHOTT
SENIOR LEAD PASTOR, MERCY CULTURE CHURCH

Christians will never get in trouble for having a private faith. Christians will always get in trouble for having a public faith. If your faith is only private, you have picked a fight with God. If your faith is also public, you are picking a fight with the world. The question is not, Will you get in trouble? The question is, Will you get in the right kind of trouble? That is the theme of this book, and it is much needed in our day of decline, when it seems everyone but the Christians have come out of the closet.

—MARK DRISCOLL
FOUNDING AND SENIOR PASTOR, TRINITY CHURCH AND REAL FAITH MINISTRY

We have a generation of trembling pastors who entered the pulpit expecting peace but finding a raging spiritual war. Pastor Johnson's timely work, *(Un)Embarrassed of Jesus*, closes the gap, equipping leaders to stand strong.

—LUCAS MILES
SENIOR DIRECTOR, TPUSA FAITH; BEST-SELLING AUTHOR, *PAGAN THREAT*

Travis Johnson has written the wake-up call the church desperately needs. Too many believers have traded bold discipleship for comfortable distance, and this book exposes that deadly compromise with unflinching clarity. Using Peter's powerful transformation as a blueprint, Travis maps out the path from lukewarm faith to fearless devotion. If you're tired of playing it safe with Jesus, this book will ignite a fire in your heart that can't be contained.

—MIKE SIGNORELLI
LEAD PASTOR, V1 CHURCH

Pastors willing to engage culture with truth are rare. Travis Johnson has given us all a poignant reminder to stand up for truth. It is a timely and transformational message for all who will hear it.

—ALLEN JACKSON
SENIOR PASTOR, WORLD OUTREACH CHURCH

Pastor Travis Johnson has proved time and again that he's not embarrassed by any word or aspect of the Scriptures, no matter what the culture says or what it might cost him. Telling the truth in a world of lies is dangerous business, and it requires courage. This book will give believers the courage necessary to proclaim the lordship of Christ, completely unembarrassed!

—BRYAN DAWSON
FOUNDER AND CEO, 1819 NEWS

I'm so righteously proud of my friend Pastor Travis Johnson as he continues to stand for truth and tell the uncompromising message of Jesus to a world that needs to hear it.

—JONI LAMB
COFOUNDER AND PRESIDENT, DAYSTAR TELEVISION NETWORK

(Un)Embarrassed of Jesus is more than a book—it's a prophetic call to courage for a generation on the precipice of compromise. My friend Pastor Travis Johnson doesn't just write about standing for truth; he's done it. When his prayer over the Mobile City Council sparked outrage and personal attacks, he didn't retreat—he stood boldly for Christ with conviction and grace.

In this book, Pastor Travis exposes the subtle ways believers can follow Jesus at a distance, like Peter in the courtyard, and challenges us instead to walk in unflinching loyalty to our Savior. His words are not theory; they're forged in the heat of real persecution and refined by genuine faith.

I know Travis personally—his integrity is tested, his courage proven, and his love for the gospel undeniable. Every pastor, every believer, and every parent raising kids in today's confused culture needs this book. (Un)Embarrassed of Jesus will strengthen your resolve, deepen your devotion, and remind you that we are not called to blend in—we are called to boldly stand out for Christ.

—JEFF SCHWARZENTRAUB
SENIOR PASTOR, BRAVE CHURCH

I can't think of anyone better suited than Travis Johnson to write this book. It is a trumpet call to just the kind of bold, muscular, and fearless Christianity so needed today. I strongly recommend this book.

—MARK RUTLAND
FOUNDER AND DIRECTOR, NATIONAL INSTITUTE OF
CHRISTIAN LEADERSHIP

In an age of compromise, when many pastors are caving in to the pressure of compromise, Travis Johnson is unashamed of the powerful truth found in the Holy Bible. Now is the time for other Christians to stand boldly and fearlessly for truth. This book will both challenge and motivate you to stand and not bow.

—MIKE FORBIS
FOUNDER AND CEO, F&F CONSTRUCTION

Travis Johnson lives his life out loud, unembarrassed by his faith, his stand for righteousness, and his love for family as God intended it to be. In this book, Travis challenges each of us to stand up, speak out, and make a difference in the world in which we live by following the example of the greatest difference maker in history, Jesus Himself.

—BRUCE DEEL
FOUNDER AND CEO, CITY OF REFUGE AND MEN OPPOSING
SEX TRAFFICKING

Travis writes as a pastor who has lived this book. His obedience to Christ's call has been transformative in the lives of those who go to Pathway Church, as well as in the city, state, and country that he dwells in. His faithfulness has moved him from the pulpit to city hall, and to the very halls of the White House. He is living proof that God blesses an unembarrassed faith.

—STEVEN WHITLOW
LEAD PASTOR, REDEMPTION CHURCH

We live in the United States of America, proclaimed as the land of the free and home of the brave, yet it takes courage and tenacity to stand and preach this great gospel in the face of an emotionally charged society that is moved so easily by feelings and ungodly opinions. Nevertheless, it is incredible to see my fellow brother in Christ, Travis Johnson, stand boldly and fearlessly proclaim Jesus Christ is still the only way, the truth, and the life!

—APOSTLE DAVID R. BRINSON
SENIOR PASTOR, EIGHTH DAY CHURCH

It is my honor to endorse Pastor Travis Johnson and his book, *(Un)Embarrassed of Jesus*. As the lead pastor of Pathway Church in Mobile, Alabama, Pastor Travis exemplifies unwavering conviction, compassion, and Christ-centered passion—consistently inspiring believers to live boldly and authentically for Jesus in a world that often rewards silence.

I believe this book will not only challenge readers to stand unashamed of the gospel but also ignite a movement of courage and faith, empowering many to live out their callings with boldness, humility, and grace for the glory of God.

—FRED TOKE, PsyD
COO, PEOPLE FOR CARE & LEARNING

In the current world of a growing and vibrant Christianity, God has raised up a powerful voice in Travis Johnson. His keen insight into the cultural, political, and spiritual landscape of the times is so phenomenal that one can readily see that he has been divinely inspired by God. His new book, *(Un)Embarrassed of Jesus*, is a powerful treatise of truth that will most certainly impact this generation for Christ.

—DAVID M. GRIFFIS, DDIV
FATHER IN THE FAITH, TREASURED FRIEND, AND OG

Travis is an incredible individual with a powerful anointing to marry politics and successful pastoral finesse in a way that speaks loudly to the cultural needs of our confused contemporary society. We need to hear him and support his endeavors to give our personal perspectives a right side up—great to have him on my friends list.

—DICK BRASWELL
SENIOR PASTOR, LIFE CHURCH; FOUNDER, FAITH ACADEMY

Redemptive leaders are called to stand between light and dark, life and death, declaring words of wholeness in the face of the hiss of the next deception. Secular culture will often label those voices as polarizing, when in fact that voice is declaring the bridge on which the broken and blind can cross over. I know of no one who more unswervingly stands on that bridge of hope, boldly defending it with certain clarity, than Travis Johnson. Unashamed, unembarrassed, driven by mercy—we need this book!

—TOM STERBENS
LEAD PASTOR, NEW HOPE CHURCH; FOUNDER, COVENANT
COMMUNITY MINISTRIES

A message that is bold, clear, strong, courageous—for such a time as this. This is not the time for a confused or conflicted church. I know you will be encouraged by my friend Pastor Travis Johnson.

—TIM CLINTON, EdD, LPC, LMFT
PRESIDENT, AMERICAN ASSOCIATION OF CHRISTIAN
COUNSELORS

In a time when culture is shifting and belief systems are being compromised, voices of bold faith are desperately needed. That is exactly what Pastor Travis Johnson calls us to in *(Un)Embarrassed of Jesus*—a challenge to live courageously, stand faithfully, and declare Christ without hesitation.

—TONY STEWART
FIRST ASSISTANT GENERAL OVERSEER, CHURCH OF GOD,
CLEVELAND, TENNESSEE

Travis Johnson is a bold and uncompromising leader who proclaims the gospel with clarity and conviction. Unmoved by the shifting winds of culture, he stands as a living testimony to Paul's declaration that we are not ashamed of the gospel of Jesus Christ (Rom. 1:16).

In an age when many spiritual voices retreat from engaging with the moral and cultural challenges of our time, Travis applies his faith courageously and consistently to real-world issues. His message calls believers to live unembarrassed, unafraid, and unwavering in their allegiance to Christ.

—JOEY GRIZZLE
LEAD PASTOR, BUFORD CHURCH OF GOD

(Un)Embarrassed of Jesus by Pastor Travis Johnson is a clarion call for the church to rise with boldness and stand unashamed for Christ in a culture desperate for truth. With conviction and compassion, Pastor Travis reminds us that the unadulterated truth of God is the only hope strong enough to heal and transform a world in desperate need of Jesus. This book ignites believers to carry the light of Christ into the most challenging and hopeless places with unshakable courage and boldness.

—COLEMAN BAILEY
MISSIONARY, SERVING ORPHANS WORLDWIDE; COFOUNDER,
CHILDREN'S REFUGE

Pastor Travis Johnson's boldness, fearless preaching, and unwavering stand for righteousness are exactly what this generation needs. In a time when many have deconstructed their faith, his voice carries the conviction and clarity that can reconstruct hearts, restore truth, and rebuild lives upon the unshakable foundation of God's Word. *(Un)Embarrassed of Jesus* is a call for courage, repentance, and revival in our nation and in leaders.

—KELLY LOHRKE
LEAD PASTOR, THE CURE CHURCH; CHURCH PLANTER;
AUTHOR

(Un)Embarrassed of Jesus by Pastor Travis Johnson is a bold and inspiring call to live out your faith with courage and conviction. With powerful stories and practical truth, Travis challenges readers to step out of fear and into fearless witness. His passion for sharing Jesus—on the page and in everyday life—makes this book a must-read for anyone ready to stand unembarrassed.

—WESLEY WEATHERFORD
SENIOR PASTOR, OASIS CHURCH AT HEPHZIBAH

Too many writers share their theories. But this book is filled with practical truths. This is a book in which the author has proved these truths by both scriptural proof and experience. This book will challenge you.

—DWIGHT ALLEN
LEAD PASTOR, THE ANCHOR CHURCH

Pastor Travis Johnson's new book powerfully articulates the call to follow Jesus as a catalyst for world transformation. He challenges readers to embrace their role in making a difference through faith and service. This inspiring guide is essential for anyone eager to impact their community and the world for Christ.

—RAUL MOLINA
LEAD PASTOR, CORNERSTONE CHRISTIAN CHURCH, MIAMI,
FLORIDA

not assume any responsibility for third-party websites or their content.

For more resources like this, visit MyCharismaShop.com.

Cataloging-in-Publication Data is on file with the Library of Congress.
International Standard Book Number: 978-1-63641-512-3
E-book ISBN: 978-1-63641-513-0

1 2025
Printed in the United States of America

Most Charisma Media products are available at special quantity discounts for bulk purchase for sales promotions, premiums, fund-raising, and educational needs. For details, call us at (407) 333-0600 or visit our website at charismamedia.com.

To Pathway Church: Your faith, love, and unwavering support light the way. This book is for you, with gratitude for your lives, your witness, and our journey together. Being your pastor since 2016 has been a great joy and honor.

CONTENTS

Foreword by Jentezen Franklin........ xvii

Preface xxi

Part I: Following at a Distance

Chapter 1   Embarrassed of Jesus....................1

Chapter 2   Losing Sight of Jesus 21

Chapter 3   The Deadly Drift 37

Part II: Denial and Deconstruction

Chapter 4   The Deconstruction of Simon Peter 71

Chapter 5   Reaching the Low Point 89

Chapter 6   The Prodigal Church Is Coming to
Its Senses 109

Part III: Following Jesus, Changing the World

Chapter 7   Hope for the Church 129

Chapter 8   Empowered Faith 145

Chapter 9   Courageous, Contagious Faith.......... 161

Chapter 10 World-Changing Faith 175

A Personal Invitation from the Author 189

Notes.................................191

Acknowledgments 193

About the Author 197

FOREWORD

WHEN I FIRST heard that his book was titled *(Un)Embarrassed of Jesus,* I knew it was the perfect time and the absolute right topic for Pastor Travis Johnson. Travis is a friend, and knowing his heart for Jesus and his prophetic courage, it is no surprise that he would write such a bold book and that it would carry an urgent message for our times. This is no mere collection of ideas; it is a rallying cry for believers everywhere. It is my honor to pen this foreword, believing these pages could very well carry the necessary sparks to set the church ablaze in this critical hour.

When Jesus said, "If anyone desires to come after Me, let him deny himself, and take up his cross daily, and follow Me" (Luke 9:23, NKJV), He was not making a suggestion; He was issuing a call to radical devotion. Today's church has too many folks who, like Peter, miss this reality. They follow Jesus but from a safe enough distance to avoid the difficulty that comes from being a Christ follower in an antichrist world. Travis refuses to let anyone stay there. With the heart of a pastor and prophetic zeal, he challenges us to throw off embarrassment and draw near to Jesus.

This message resonates with me. For decades, I have preached that the nearer you are to Christ, the more transformative your faith becomes. The closer you find yourself to Him, the more His life shapes yours. Travis lays this out clearly, contrasting the weak faith and fading testimony of those who keep their distance with the world-changing fire of those who pursue Christ whole-heartedly. I've seen this reality play out more times than I can count: distant followers losing their faith while those who press in see the impossible become reality.

Travis does more than offer commentary or diagnose the issues. In this book readers will find answers for how to close the gap and experience what it means to follow closely. In a world that beckons believers to apathy and tame faith, a world where Christians seem to be apologetic about the hard truths of the gospel, Travis reminds us that Jesus never called us to blend in. Ours is a call to be salt, to be light, to be unembarrassed.

Using personal stories, practical insight, and scriptural wisdom, Travis has penned a useful and edifying book that digs into tough issues and provides much-needed guidance. More than theory, this book flows from a life that has walked out the lessons in its pages. I've prayed for Pastor Travis when he was a teenage boy, his young soul hungry for more of God. I've stood with him and prayed together over the president and our nation. I have watched as the young man I prayed for all those years ago followed Jesus closely. And as a result of his devotion, he has found favor with God, becoming a change agent for the kingdom. That's the boldness he's calling us to.

Here you will find the reflections and lessons of a life shaped by choosing God-focus over earthly distraction, passionate love over indifference, and difficult truth over easy silence. This kind of faith is the kind we all need, the kind that does more than endure. It impacts. I join Travis in this message: When someone follows Jesus closely, it changes more than their own life; it elevates families, communities, nations, and the world.

(Un)Embarrassed of Jesus is a timely challenge for the church. The church is in desperate need of believers who are not afraid to lift Jesus high, regardless of what it may cost them.

Travis has given us a tool to sharpen our faith, awaken our spirits, and strengthen our witness. As you read, I pray you'll feel the Holy Spirit pulling you closer to Jesus, the way He's been pulling Travis since his teenage days. This isn't about perfection—it's about pursuit. When we pursue Jesus with all we've got, His power flows through us in ways we can't fathom.

So let this book shake you, inspire you, and light a fire in you. Travis has poured his soul into these words, and I believe God's going to use them to stir something mighty. Follow Jesus closely—don't settle for the sidelines—and watch what He does through you.

—JENTEZEN FRANKLIN
SENIOR PASTOR, FREE CHAPEL
NEW YORK TIMES BEST-SELLING AUTHOR

PREFACE

As a pastor of twenty-five years, I've engaged with others enough to see patterns loop around in the lives of scores of people. The pattern recognition coupled with experience and a clear path in Scripture detailing the outcome of bold, unembarrassed faith is prominent enough that I wanted to share it with you as both a caution and an encouragement.

What I've witnessed is a strong uptake for those who are bold, and timid, passive, failed outcomes for those who lag, following Jesus from a distance. There is no viable middle way. There is only bold faith or no faith. Repeatedly, we see in the Scriptures that passive faith leads to abandoned faith. Jesus said in Revelation 3:15-16, "I know your deeds, that you are neither cold nor hot. I wish you were either one or the other! So, because you are lukewarm—neither hot nor cold—I am about to spit you out of my mouth."

Our words and our deeds will be congruent. Either our words will match our deeds, or our deeds will match our words, bringing us to bold faith or a functionally lost faith.

Your bold faith is your best contribution to God and to your fellow man. No one will march to the beat of an uncertain drummer. You must know where you're going and boldly go there. Leading passively or timidly will take you and everyone else nowhere.

Going boldly is a life of joy, adventure, and empowerment in God. Surround yourself with like-minded people who are unembarrassed of Jesus, and go!

A QUICK NOTE ABOUT ONE OF THE BOOK'S FEATURES

As you make your way through this journey, you'll notice QR codes like the following one placed throughout the book. These aren't just extra features—they're designed to keep you connected. Each code will link you to resources, encouragement, and a community of people walking the same *(Un)Embarrassed of Jesus* journey.

Whenever you see one, open your phone's camera, scan the code, and tap the link that appears. It's that simple. By doing so, you'll not only gain tools to strengthen your faith but also join the (Un)Embarrassed Tribe—a growing family committed to standing boldly for Jesus.

So don't just read this book—experience it. Stay connected, stay resourced, and stay unembarrassed.

Scan the QR code or visit bit.ly/
42k1hIm to connect with us and
join the (Un)Embarrassed Tribe.

PART I

FOLLOWING AT A DISTANCE

Chapter 1

EMBARRASSED OF JESUS

*So they arrested him and led him to the high
priest's home. And Peter followed at a distance.*
—LUKE **22:54**, NLT

"**W**HAT NOW?"

He had never been this torn before. Should he stay to watch? Should he try to make eye contact with Jesus, signaling that he had not abandoned Him?

Should he march to the center of the courtyard, stare the leaders of the Sanhedrin in the eye, and declare that he had something to say? Should he bear witness that Jesus was in fact the Son of God? Should he testify that he had heard the voice of God from heaven declaring it so, that he had seen Elijah and Moses talking with his beloved teacher?

They would kill him too.

Maybe he should slip into the back alleys of Jerusalem and find those among the anti-Roman zealotry to mount an armed rescue. No, that could not be right. Just hours ago Jesus scolded him for using his sword to resist the authorities. Besides, they stood no chance against the temple guards or the Roman detachment, doubly so while its ranks were reinforced to handle the Passover crowds.

Should he run? Would they be coming for him, his brother, and the other disciples? If he left now, he could get out of the city before a manhunt began in earnest.

That was the answer. He would flee. He could be out of Judea by tomorrow and in a few days be back on his boat. Perhaps, if he kept his head down, paid his taxes, and was a good citizen, his "religious" phase would pass from memory. One thing was certain: He could not risk staying in this place. After all, what good was a dead husband to his wife?

Coming here was a huge mistake. How could he get out of the courtyard? There, an opening in the crowd. Run.

"Hey, I know you!" a voice nearby spoke, pausing his flight before it began. "You are one of His students."

Looking down, he mumbled what sounded like, "You are mistaken, friend," and turned back toward his escape route.

The gap had closed. A man and woman—pilgrims by the look of the dust-laden packs they carried—stood in his way, craning their necks for a better view of Caiaphas confronting Jesus inside. Shoving past them, he took a few more steps. Someone back in the room yelled something about blasphemy. His breath came in short, rapid succession. He had to move faster.

It was unfeasible to navigate this jostling mass of humanity while keeping his face turned toward the ground, but he could not afford to be recognized again. What was he thinking? He was a fisherman. He had a family to feed. Why did he ever allow himself to get caught up in this?

Yes, from that first conversation with Jesus, he had never been the same. There could be no denying that. There could also be no denying that he had seen things that could be explained only by the hand of God. His own mother-in-law had been healed. He had said, he had even believed, that Jesus was the Son of God.

No matter—he signed up to follow a teacher, not die for a cause. Believing was one thing. Arrests and trials were something totally different. If he did die, it was going to be with a sword in his hand, not sniveling before an executioner like some common criminal.

"Aren't you one of the Jesus people?" A rough hand grabbed his arm. He spun to face the speaker. A mountain of a man looked down on him.

"I've seen you around with Him. You were in Jericho with Him just a few days ago. There was a pretty big crowd, but you were right there beside Him."

A few heads turned their way.

"You've had too much to drink tonight," he replied. "I've never seen Him before in my life."

Those nearest in the crowd turned away from the interrogation, forming a semicircle around the two men.

"Yes, yes, I know you," another voice said.

He knew that voice. His eyes locked on hers. She had been around several times when Jesus was in Jerusalem. She had even given Andrew directions once.

"You are Simon. You and your brother, Andrew, you are His followers."

3

His stomach dropped. The hand on his arm tightened its grip. A temple guard looked their way. His heart pounded in his ears. Under his cloak, Peter's fingers searched for his sword.

He cursed and sneered at her. "Foolish woman. This fire must be where all the blind idiots have gathered."

Jerking free, Peter careened through the crowd, nearly running now. Seeing a doorway, he lurched through it and onto the street. Across the rooftops the first light of dawn appeared over the Mount of Olives.

And a block away, a rooster prepared to wake the world.

THE ROOSTER STILL CROWS

Bitter tears and shame were imminent, but were they inevitable? No matter how many times we revisit the story of Peter's cryptic desertions of Christ, we always seem to miss that question. We rightfully elevate this moment as an inspirational reminder that God forgives human frailty. We wisely analyze each denial, searching for clues to help us uproot the abandoning tendencies in our hearts. Yet we rarely pause to ask, Did it have to be this way?

Closer to home, we should be inquiring whether the deconversion of those around us is avoidable. Your social media feed is probably a lot like mine, invaded by a steady drip of the deconstructed declaring their newfound "truths" and denying foundational tenets of Christian thought, doctrine, and practice.

And by *deconstructed* I do not mean to point out those of us who have or will read the Bible afresh and pose healthy questions for our Christian traditions and assumptions.

Rather, I am talking about those who have bought into a cultural full-court press that is pushing a complete departure from faith by way of a slow rejection of biblical truth, absolute truth, and the authority of the Scriptures in favor of postmodern philosophy and moral relativism.

From Christian artists to the person you sat beside in children's ministry to some of the church leaders you once looked up to, something has happened. People who once declared their love for God, many of whom really believed, have made head-spinning changes in their beliefs and practices.

Not all their stories are the same. Some completely abandon all faith in God, becoming militantly opposed to all things Christian. These are the family members who get triggered by saying grace at Thanksgiving and want to convince you that the holiday has more to do with the oppression of vulnerable peoples by an evil Eurocentric empire than it does a grateful group of Christians demonstrating thankfulness to God for having survived the bitter New England winter after fleeing religious oppression. They show up in the social media comments on your invitation to Easter services and declare it a veiled attempt to oppress freethinkers through the opiate of religion.

Some have deconstructed because of unresolved doubts and the church failing to provide adequate answers to their uncertainties. Someone talked them out of their faith, and now they want to talk you out of yours. Others have experienced church hurt and have not healed. In rejecting the institution they blame for their pain, they have rejected God Himself.

Whatever their origin stories, they frequently become the most clamorous opposition to all things Christian. You will find them as the most vocal voices in the push to remove prayer from the public sphere, Christian thought from legislative processes, and Christian people from public influence. They are not simply former believers; they are antibelief.

A few years ago I was invited to offer an invocation for the Mobile City Council. As the pastor of Pathway Church, which has sustained a growing footprint in the city for many years, the invitation was not unusual. A local pastor praying before a civic event in Alabama is not exactly newsworthy. It is more surprising if you get a group of Alabamians together and there is no opening prayer. Prayer is part of life here.

That day, I stepped to the podium, thanked the mayor and council for the opportunity to be there, and proceeded to pray a simple pastoral prayer over my city. I acknowledged God as creator, sustainer, and supplier of all good gifts. I prayed for the members of the council by name, for God to help them carry out their duties, for protection of our children, and for God to lead our city to knowledge of Christ, who loves and redeems sinners. You can imagine my surprise when that moment of prayer became the catalyst for spiritual war in Mobile.

Anti-Christian journalists and activist organizations seized on a few sentences of my prayer. They took particular umbrage with my praying for "protection of the children of Mobile who are inundated and targeted by harmful agendas." I never named a particular group or offered any explanation of "harmful agendas" and prayed specifically for godly governance of "all of our [Mobile's] citizens."[1] The facts were irrelevant.

My prayer was labeled anti-LGBTQ, and the proverbial (and probably not-so-proverbial) calls for my head began.

After my public prayer, I was called names too vulgar to reprint.

I became the subject of news articles, drawing the ire of journalists and organizations on the state and national level. Almost all my social media interactions drew fire from people I had never met, many of whom had never been to Mobile. My family was doxed, and my wife, who had merely been present at the council meeting, endured public ridicule. I was called names too vulgar to reprint and had to come to grips with being the face of a legal, spiritual, and political battle.

In that moment, I had few clear options. I could back down. I could offer some "clarifying statement." I could call for a meeting with some local LGBTQ leader and let the world know I was terribly sorry for any confusion or hurt that had been caused by my lack of clarity. I could embark on a public relations campaign, assuring the city that my deeply held personal beliefs were indeed so deep and so personal that I would never dare let them out in public again.

But I could do none of those things.

I could not be embarrassed of Jesus.

Some of the response was to be expected. It was not astonishing to see that the people who supported drag queens dancing in front of our children were opposed to my position. It was certainly not groundbreaking that certain media outlets were less than flattering. The Freedom From Religion Foundation acted exactly as I would have expected. Other secular, leftist activist groups howled with their typical angst. The eye-opening part of this was that so many of those vilifying me were former Christians—especially former evangelical Christians. They had walked away from the faith but had grown obsessed with returning to attack the church.

The story of my prayer spread, and the comments section of my social media became a battleground. The *culture warrior* moniker is frequently used as a pejorative to malign believers who take any sort of public position on the moral questions of the moment. Anyone who thinks Evangelicals are too aggressive in their interactions has never seen the vitriol that pours out of the leftist, humanist, atheist crowd.

Further inflaming the sensitivities of my God-hating critics was that, by Providence, the invitation to pray before the city council meeting had occurred just before "pride" month, to which I was responding with a series of sermons addressing sexuality and gender from a biblical worldview. There was plenty for the descending mob to react to, and react they did.

For decades, antichrist forces have been perfecting the art of arriving en masse to voice displeasure and apply pressure against any attempts to advance kingdom ideology. If biblical Christians and conservatives had half the dedication to show up for our causes, our nation would be in a much better place. Of course, when you are the people running small businesses, building communities, feeding the poor, and prioritizing family, it becomes a little more difficult to drop everything and show up for the latest outrage caucus.

The internet has taken the world of constant protest to new heights. Now you don't even have to change your Cheeto-stained shirt or leave your mom's basement to let the world know just how right you are on every topic from the anatomy of a "birthing person" to the injustice of the system so oppressive, almost anyone can make it out of poverty by following two or three simple guidelines for life. Instead, you can visit your favorite subreddit and be told by the hive mind just what you should be angry about today, and you can even tap a link where you can join the revolution. Marx would be proud. He, the ever-noncontributing loafer who thought his writing so profound that he should be subsidized while spewing ineffectual drivel, has been replicated by millions of online profiles complete with multigender pronouns and labor slogans parroted by people who have never done any real work.

If biblical Christians and conservatives had half the dedication to show up for our causes, our nation would be in a much better place.

The fact that there was an angry horde of fanatics asserting the most radical elements of their LGBTQ agenda was not surprising. I knew the internet worked like this. While being the target of the woke mob was not something I sought out, it certainly was not something completely unexpected. Looking back, I'm not even surprised that so many who had rejected Christianity and theism were coming after me. But there was one group that was heartbreaking to see.

Among the battery of complaints and litany of reasons for offense was a remarkable number of comments by people who identified as formerly conservative Christians. Some of the most persistent voices against me were those whose comments included how they previously attended a "church like this" or were raised in "fundie" homes. The Christians-turned-atheists who had shown up to fight over a public prayer in a Bible Belt state were one thing, but this was something else entirely.

Apostate churches are not new. Many have turned from truth. In my lifetime countless ministers have been derelict in their duty to declare the whole counsel of God, and entire denominations have defected from biblical orthodoxy. Others had been far from faithful long before I began in ministry. However, when walking through this tough season, I became keenly aware that the rot was deeper and far more widespread than I had ever imagined.

I was not naive. I have always tried to stay informed of what is happening in the world around me. Like many other Christians, I have seen Christianity being steadily pushed into a corner in our country. Certainly, the decline of Christian influence had its landmark moments. There was the removal of prayer from schools, the proliferation of no-fault divorce, and the original *Roe v. Wade* decision. Looking around, it was easy to see that stable Christian values were steadily eroding from our culture.

Pearl clutching is not my thing. I grew up in South Florida. I am so Miami that, despite a decade in Alabama, if you cut me, I'd still bleed *café con leche*. I pastored for years in a city that is not known for a conservative social milieu—Miami is not the Bible Belt. Sinful, broken people are going to live sinful lives, driven by their brokenness. Of this I am aware.

While I harbored no expectation of a Christianized mainstream culture, it was still unsettling to see the rapidity at which society was casting off most biblical norms and values. Secularization of our thought was having devastating results. As we threw off the ways of God, the moral lawgiver, we lost the benefits that come from the structure provided by moral imperatives. It follows that institutions designed by God—namely, the family, government, and church—began to suffer from this rejection of absolutes.

Since the middle of the twentieth century, America has been on a journey to release itself from structures deemed antiquated and restrictive. In the name of freedom, we rejected God's ideas of sexuality and decency. In search of success, we sacrificed family at the altar of gain. In our attempts at tolerance, we rejected the idea that some things should be promoted as good and others resisted as evil. As arbiters of personal truth, we bought into the lie that there will be no real consequences. After all, God exists only for those who believe in Him, so who will judge the rest of us?

When Lewis Carroll's protagonist, Alice, made her decision to imbibe, the author wrote, "If you drink much from a bottle marked 'poison,' it is almost certain to disagree with you, sooner or later."[2] At the time of my writing, the last twenty years in America have proved the novelist to be prophetic. As a pastor I have been right in the middle of distraught lives in that terrible moment when the social poison begins to disagree.

Not only have I walked with people through terrible moments brought on by the deterioration of society around us; I have also witnessed a shift in the way people like me are viewed by many around us, including those who have gained governmental authority.

We have seen attacks on religious liberty. In unprecedented fashion the United States government actively engaged in lawfare persecution of Christians for doing what they have always done—attempting to live in a manner consistent with historic Christian doctrine. Hobby Lobby, a national arts and crafts company founded by evangelical businessman and philanthropist David Green, was forced to sue—eventually winning a historic decision by the United States Supreme Court—to escape being forced to financially support the murder of unborn children. The Little Sisters of the Poor faced millions of dollars in fines because they dared to stand on centuries-old Catholic positions regarding contraception.

Christians, at least those who attempted to live

their lives according to a biblical worldview, were being pushed further and further toward the margins. While the entertainment and media industries have always operated with a measure of irreverence toward Christian values, open hostility was new territory. In movies, television, music, and network and cable news, any tendency toward conservative social values began being painted as extreme fundamentalism, Christian nationalism, and a danger to our freedom. Mockery and derision came from national-level politics, where salt-of-the-earth people were ridiculed as "clinging to their Bibles and guns" and labeled as "deplorable." Many once-respected legacy media outlets produced weekly, sometimes daily, attacks on Christians—especially on Evangelicals. A nation with the thread of Christianity woven through its story was turning not just away from God but against Him.

Something far more pernicious was happening within the church itself. Some church attenders, self-professing evangelical Christians, aligned themselves with the attacking secular voices. Much of this played out on social media. A simple post reflecting age-old Christian views would result in a comments section filled with every possible position opposing the biblical one. While their comments would sometimes include while-I-agree-with-you disclaimers, many who insisted on playing devil's advocate were quite literally doing the devil's work. These milquetoast Christians with their sloppy attempts at nuance did little more than muddy the waters and create schism by smuggling in humanistic and antichrist ideology under the auspices of "understanding" and "tolerance" and a misconstrued representation of love. Those who would dare speak against this encroachment would themselves be maligned as intolerant or mean-spirited by other Christians who prioritized unity above all.

The church has spent years seeking to be palatable at all costs. Christian institutions have been commandeered by leaders who are more concerned with being included at prestigious tables than holding fast to truth. Pulpits have been infiltrated by cowardly hirelings who would rather fill the pews with crowds sedated by a seeker-centered TED Talk than risk offending anyone with the sanctifying challenge to take up a cross and follow Christ. It has worked. These mercurial ministers, floating along on the whims of public opinion, have gained many followers. In their churches, Christ has gained precious few.

This drift has brought us to a place where many churchgoers have become a living paradox. They proclaim an allegiance to Christ while living lives that reflect precious little of His kingship. They quote the poetry and prose of Scripture for comfort but just as readily quote pop psychology and Marxist rhetoric. While claiming to love God, they trip over themselves to applaud actions and speech that are completely antithetical to His ways.

I was still pastoring in Miami when I had my first encounter with this new reality. The LGBT activists (at that time, the Q and subsequent profusion of the additional initials, numerals, and plus sign hadn't yet been added) were becoming more and more shrill around the country. Pride activities including rallies, parades, and the yearly monthlong celebration of sexual and gender confusion were beginning to gain ground. Social media was also becoming more ubiquitous, allowing for a deeper glimpse into the lives of those around us. I remember being surprised, then shocked, then appalled as I saw more and more people claiming to be followers of Christ while celebrating sin online.

Pride flags showed up in profile pictures, and Christians began to identify themselves as allies. Some did not go so far as to openly defend the LGBT movement but were quick to like and offer their congratulations on posts that ranged from gay relationship announcements to people "coming out" as homosexual. As years passed, this phenomenon would only grow. Christians—even church leaders—lauding homosexual "love" or commending the bravery of confused and broken people "finding their truth" has become all too common. But even in those early days, I could not believe what I was seeing.

Celebrating sin in the name of affirmation is a confusing prospect to onlookers—believers and unbelievers alike. It is harmfully disorienting to those we are attempting to reach with a gospel we claim is transformative. For those in the church, it runs the risk of letting them believe that such sin is not all that dangerous and that it might not even be sin at all. It is no coincidence that the more nuanced our approach becomes, the further we find ourselves from living our lives God's way. You cannot negotiate with an enemy whose only goal is to destroy you. The church is slowly finding this out.

I was growing increasingly concerned about the trends I was seeing in the church as a whole. Some in my congregation were being pulled toward affirming sin. Others were not going so far as to openly affirm or support, but they had grown quiet in the face of mounting opposition. People who were bold about almost any topic shrank back from this one. When questioned directly, pastors with public influence were saying that they had their own personal views, but it was not their place to judge the right or wrong of others' choices. Like Peter, some distanced themselves from the controversial, even claiming they did so for the righteous reason of maintaining relevance or advancing the gospel. What they failed to recognize was that a gospel with no confrontation of (and victory over) sin is not the gospel at all. They were being accepted, but they were doing so by risking the souls of the very people accepting them.

WHEN BELIEVERS DISTANCE THEMSELVES

It is difficult to understand why those who believe Jesus is Lord would try to distance themselves from Him. It is nigh impossible to grasp why these people, who believe sin is a curse that carries the penalty of death and that the saving work of Jesus can deliver from sin and its consequences (Rom. 6:23), would then attempt to avoid pointing out the disparity between the lifestyle of the saved and that of the lost. If Christianity does not offer something radically different from a life of sin, then what is the point? If the Bible is really God's prescription for a sin-sick world, then how can we so easily dismiss it? It is cognitive dissonance to be a believer but not be all in—to claim Jesus is who we say He is and then try to avoid being identified as radically His.

An alarming number of Christians today, through their affirmations, conversations, and even their own lifestyle choices, are blatantly denying connection to Christ and His Word. Like Peter, their assertions have increased in flagrance.

How did we get here?

How does a believer arrive at the place where their worldview is diametrically opposed to biblical, historical Christian teaching?

Believers are not having some sort of reverse Paul-on-the-road-to-Damascus moment. They are not abandoning long-held truth after one conversation with a woke professor or being stuck in an airport lounge while MSNBC is on. One trip down a deconstructionist YouTube rabbit hole does not lead them to purchase an LGBTQ flag or become a militant defender of drag-queen story hour. It's much subtler. They, like Peter, do not start with denial. They start by putting a little distance between themselves and Christ.

A gospel with no confrontation of sin is not the gospel at all.

When my daughter Kourtney was in the fourth grade, we had a moment that is allegorical for what is happening in the church. She was at that stage in a child's life when they are still very much a child but they want to have some independence. What they really want is to begin developing their own identity. One day as I was dropping her off at school, we made our way through the dense crowd of parents and students, and I noticed that she was beginning to get a few steps ahead. Even as I picked up my pace, I could see her weaving through the crowd, getting farther and farther ahead. As she waved and spoke to friends, I got the sense that she was intentionally putting distance between us. Hold on—was my daughter hitting that "Dad is embarrassing" stage?

I had no reason to be concerned that I would lose her. We were in Miami, a famously Latino city that was around 15 percent Caucasian. No matter how big she made the gap, there was no way I was going to lose sight of the lone blond ponytail bobbing up and down in the sea of black and brown hair. If she was worried about being identified with her daddy, she was going to need a new strategy. One look at her and the tall white guy trailing her was a dead giveaway.

It was laughable for her to think she could somehow not be known as mine. In the same way, it is preposterous for anyone with a relationship with Jesus to think they are going to navigate this world without being marked as His. You cannot have His love without His truth. You cannot seek His justice while denying His moral law. It just makes no sense.

If we are His, we are comprehensively His. Being embarrassed of Him is an impossible posture to hold. How can I tell others that Jesus can change their lives while I am ashamed to be associated with Him? Believers who shirk the reality that Christianity is different from the belief structures of this world—as well as those who hide from the moral demands of our Creator—are just as misguided as my little fourth grader. You can deny, you can seek distance, but there is no way to be discreetly His.

The 2015 *Obergefell v. Hodges* decision, in which the US Supreme Court ruled 5 to 4 that same-sex marriage was to be legal in all fifty states, was yet to happen. Homosexual marriage was not yet legal in Florida when I came face-to-face with this reality in my church. We experienced growth and saw incredible things happen in our church family. I was preaching the gospel, working as hard as I could to be innovative and inviting, and God was honoring the work by giving us exceptional growth in a city that was not known for its evangelical presence. I preached truth, even hard truth. But engaging cultural issues was not top of mind.

Then they came to tell me their news.

Two people who attended my church, people I counted as friends, informed me that they were taking a trip to New York to get married. They were both women. As they told me, I tried to gather my thoughts. They knew how our church believed. They knew what I believed. They had heard me speak about God's will for our lives in relationships and sexuality. But here they were nonetheless, preparing to solemnize a same-sex marriage.

At that moment, I had a decision to make. Up to this point, I had been a peacetime pastor. I was seeing souls saved, baptizing new converts, performing marriages, dedicating babies, and walking out the Christian life with my church family. Now everything was changing. I had seen the encroachment of insidious worldviews on social media. I had noticed believers avoiding controversial topics. I had heard whispers from time to time of people I knew who were deconstructing. But now we were entering a new space.

A decision had to be made. Christianity in America was heading toward a cliff, and not enough of us were hitting the brakes. Speaking up could split my church. We might lose everything we had worked to build. Speaking publicly might cost me friends or influence. What if I was ostracized as radical or too controversial? Was it really worth the risk?

The reality: If we avoid certain topics to not offend a seeker or to maintain our public palatability, there will never be a convenient time for the truth.

I made up my mind.

I could not be embarrassed of Jesus.

To view my "Being (Un)Embarrassed of Jesus" video, scan the QR code or visit bit.ly/3KJsqOG.

Chapter 2

LOSING SIGHT OF JESUS

Turn your eyes upon Jesus, look full in His won-
derful face, and the things of earth will grow
strangely dim, in the light of His glory and grace.
—HELEN H. LEMMEL

IT IS DIFFICULT to identify the moment it happened, this strange shift into a new realm where the church embraced the idea of Jesus but rejected the authority of His Word. Much commentary on the topic has been offered by well-heeled experts. If you buy a dozen books claiming to know what got us here, you will get a dozen different answers. Some will point to industrialization, some to neoconservative theology, and others to liberal drift in academic institutions. They would all be right.

Determining the exact moment and mechanism that have created our current situation is like a man walking in the rain and trying to discern at which moment he went from wet to soaked. In logic, there is something called the fallacy of the beard, which seeks to dismiss an argument if the concept is vague or exists on a spectrum. It is a fallacy because while we may not be able to pinpoint the moment stubble becomes a beard, we all know a beard when we see one. Furthermore, we know how a man becomes bearded; he fails to shave.

How did the church get this far from truth or even the belief that there is such a thing as absolute truth? How did we become so distant from what was once considered basic Christian morality? How do we have so-called Christian leaders deconstructing? How did "progressive Christianity" gain such a foothold? How did we get this distance between us and Jesus?

We failed to follow Him closely.

One evening, I was heading home after a long day at the office. We had been busy working on some new evangelistic efforts for the city and developing vision for the coming expansion of our church's campus. It had been a very consuming workday. I love what I do. The people, the planning, the vision casting, the strategizing, the practical stuff. And did I mention the people? I was born to be a pastor. But that day, I was ready to get home and hang out with Kelly and the kids. Every time I look away, it seems my kids grow a little more. So Kelly and I savor every moment we get with them.

While driving, I was on the phone with a friend who is also a pastor. As we were catching up on the past few weeks, I noticed that Blake, my seventeen-year-old son, was calling. Glancing at the clock, I knew he was heading home from soccer practice. This call was probably an attempt to convince me to vote for his dinner choice or to ask about hanging out with friends that weekend. Telling my friend I would call him back, I tapped the screen to take Blake's call.

"Dad, where are you?"

OK, he's probably home and hungry, I thought. Blake's six-foot, three-inch frame was filling out in his junior year, and anyone who has raised a boy, much less an athlete, knows they possess a level of ravenousness rivaling a grizzly after a long winter. I told him where I was, expecting him to moan that I needed to hurry.

"I've got a flat tire," Blake said.

"Where are you?"

"On the interstate."

I am raising a teen son. That means I fully expect him to be able to handle a flat tire. Listen, I'm not saying you should not be a member of AAA or pay for roadside assistance with your insurance. You never know what you'll need on the road. Nonetheless, there are some things a teenage boy should know how to do.

Raising a boy into a man includes instilling some of the practical knowledge a man should have. Extensive damage has been done to young men by treating them as if there were not certain man stuff they should know. One day, he's going to be called on to come through in a situation, and when that day comes, he needs to be equipped for the moment. That list certainly varies by context, but in general it includes some basic skills with his hands and at least some understanding of how to defend himself and others. Also on the list is knowing how to change a tire.

Not only does raising a man include passing on the how-to information; it also requires instilling the can-do disposition that he'll need later in life. Every man will eventually find himself in a position where no one is coming to rescue him, where he is being depended on, and where what must be done is difficult. When that time comes, if no one has ever let him navigate hardship, he is going to be overwhelmed—leading to failure or, worse, surrender.

Blake being on the side of the road with a flat tire at age seventeen was not something that sent me into panic mode. He was a big boy. I'd taught him how to change a tire. My initial thought was that it looked like dinner would be a little late for the goalie tonight.

"Sounds like you have a job to do, son. Welcome to Manhood 101." If his misfortune had occurred on most other roads, that would have been my play. But his being on the side of Interstate 65 was a different story. Throw in the fact that the narrow shoulder was hardly condu-cive to changing a tire, his Mustang not being able to pull up on an embankment to get clear of the roadway, and the sinking sun meaning he would be on the busy highway in the dark, and it was a recipe for something to go wrong.

"I'm on my way," I said as I changed lanes and steered onto the ramp of the next exit. If all went well, I could get to him in a few minutes and we could all get home in time for dinner.

"Dad, I've got some more bad news," Blake added

before I disconnected the call. "It looks like my spare is flat too."

Nice. Dinner and time on the deck were becoming an illusion.

There were only a few miles between where I was and where Blake had pulled to the side of the road. The evening traffic was at its typical level of busyness but moving at a steady pace. It did not take me long to reach the spot and pull in behind his Mustang. I activated my hazard lights as Blake walked back to my truck.

The crippled car was parked in a terrible spot to leave for long. The flat spare tire really created a predicament. Not a great situation, but I couldn't be too frustrated. I mean, who checks their spare tire? We had to decide whether we needed to tow the car or remove the wheel and tire to find a repair shop. I whispered a prayer and invoked my everything's-going-to-be-all-right, Dad-is-here smile.

Just as Blake started to jump in my truck so we could talk without the roar of traffic, another truck pulled into the grass on the other side of the barrier beside our vehicles.

"Hey, do you guys need some help?"

We could barely hear the driver over the roar of passing semis. He exited his truck and started making his way toward us. I got out and walked toward the barrier, noticing that this fella's truck bed was filled with tires. He introduced himself as the owner of a local tire shop. Things were looking up.

In just a few minutes, the offending tire was off Blake's car and in the back of the good Samaritan's truck. The tire shop owner had his son with him as well. It was a real father-son activity day out there on the berm.

We decided we would follow the shop owner in my truck, replace the tire, then bring it back to install on Blake's car. The sun was dropping behind the horizon. We would be arriving home later than we wanted, but the arrival of this help had still saved much time, not to mention the money saved by not needing a tow. We pulled out to follow the tire truck, grateful for how things were working out.

As we tried to enter traffic, a gap grew between us and the truck we were trying to follow. If you're ever in Mobile, I have a challenge for you. Count trucks. You cannot count that high or that fast. There are trucks everywhere here, and I was driving one too. I was never more aware of that fact than at this moment. I also quickly realized just how hard it is to tell black from blue and even from red when a truck is far enough away at dusk.

This guy had Blake's wheel and tire in the back of his truck. It wasn't like we could just decide to go to another tire shop. We could not lose track of him. I had to find our good Samaritan.

"There he is," I said more to myself than Blake, who was staring at his phone, oblivious that I had almost lost his wheel.

A few hundred feet ahead, I spotted the truck taking the long Government Boulevard exit. It looked like he was turning right off the exit. I stepped on the accelerator, the Hemi engine growled, and the gap started to close. There were several vehicles between us, but that was OK. We would be there in no time.

Blake and I talked about soccer practice. He had been developing as a soccer player and was beginning to generate buzz in the recruiting circuit. That day was a good day at practice for him. As I drove, the conversation wandered through other areas. We talked about the car, his schoolwork load, and even some construction on a Dave & Buster's we passed. As we headed out of the city limits, I thought how time had flown by. Just a few years ago, Blake had been a boy, adventurous and engaging, but a boy nonetheless. Here I was riding with a young man on the edge of some great moments in life. Wow, I was blessed.

Wait a second! Why were we heading out of the city limits?

"Blake, I don't know where this guy is going." I sped up, watching as we drew closer to the truck.

"Dad, I don't think that's the right truck."

"No way," I replied. But my son was right.

Somehow in the confusion of getting into traffic, or following at a distance on the interstate, or making a wrong decision at the exit, I had gotten behind the wrong truck. I got so caught up in conversation that I failed to notice I was being led astray.

"Blake, what was the name of that tire shop?"

"Um..." He was drawing a blank.

Apparently, in this case the apple was placed directly beneath the tree. In the rush on the side of the highway, neither of us had thought to take note of the name of the tire shop. After all, we were going to be following him; we did not need to know where he was going. Now instead of being where we needed to be, we were off course.

How did we get here? Much like the current state of our society and our churches, I could point to one moment or to many. Was it when we merged into traffic? Was it the lack of familiarity with the person we were following? Was it all the side talk and roadside distractions? The answer is yes to every question. We found ourselves miles from where we needed to be, with no idea of where we were going, because we had been poor followers. I had not followed closely enough.

FOLLOWING AT A DISTANCE

Things move so fast on the interstate. At seventy miles an hour, you can cover the length of a basketball court in the amount of time your eyes close for a sneeze. Trying to reenter traffic from the roadside that day, the cars and trucks screaming by were a reminder of just how fast the world moves on a highway. I lost sight of my guide before I even got started.

We live in a rapidly moving world. Innovation acceleration, the proliferation of technology, and the overwhelming amount of available information make it feel as if the ground is literally shifting beneath our feet. A few decades ago our church's biggest concern was whether song words should be on the wall or in a hymnal. I was a radical because our church baptized at the beach and held services in a theater. The idea of a church meeting in a secular setting was foreign and therefore dangerous. It seems like yesterday we trying to plan for adequate male

I lost sight of my guide before I even got started.

and female separation on youth retreats. Now youth pastors are being told by parents that Johnny wants to pee in the girls' restroom.

Have you listened to young people talk? What are they saying? Who knows? It changes every few months. I won't even include any references to particular words because they will have changed in the few months between the writing and publishing of this book. The deeper question is, Have you heard what they deal with in their schools, online, and even in youth group? The world is moving fast.

Kids used to sneak a cigarette in high school. Then it was middle school. Now our elementary school students are vaping. If that sounds destructive, think how terrible it is for developing minds to be exposed to hardcore pornography at younger and younger ages. Throw in major media making sure there is a disproportionate number of LGBTQ relationships in every movie or TV show, and a river of TikTok and YouTube influencers steering the thoughts of our next generations, and you'll realize that this pace of change is only going to increase.

Parents, pastors, and Christian educators and leaders must recognize that the world is moving too fast for us to let there be any distance between our young people and Jesus. If they are not bumper-to-bumper, they're going to lose sight before they even get started. Better yet, to use an Alabama idea, we have to find a way to get a logging chain from the lead vehicle to the follower. Our young people have to have their hearts stitched to Jesus' before they enter the fast-moving flow of life.

The same goes for entering any new season. Starting a marriage, launching a new career, or stepping into ministry all have the same requirement. In the flow of life, it's hard to follow Jesus closely if you let yourself start out too casually. One day, you'll look up, and the gap will be huge.

Thankfully, the Scriptures teach us that God's mercies are new every morning and we can rejoice in His faithfulness (Lam. 3:22–23). Maybe you did not start out following closely. Every day is a new opportunity to get close to God, to lock in that Holy Spirit logging chain before pulling into traffic. Set your life with routines that will make sure you are as close as you can be before launching into the fast-moving day or week.

I could have made up for the distance I lost starting that journey. The other driver was not trying to get away. I did not speed up or attempt to weave through traffic because I thought I had my eye on his vehicle. From a distance, it seemed I was on the right track. So I just went with the flow...and wound up way off course.

A false perception of the moment can have disastrous results. Peter did not have kingdom vision on the night of Christ's arrest. His own personality motivated his reaction in the arrest encounter. In that moment, he allowed himself to settle for following from a distance. Ultimately, his misunderstanding of Christ's mission led to him outright denying their relationship.

Believers must be aware that whether any distance from the Lord is created through the pace of change in life or their own disillusionment with God's plan in a particular moment, following from a distance usually results in a rejection of God. Some may say their deconstruction has not been a rejection—they might even attempt to refer to it as some deeper understanding or enlightenment. They are making Peter's mistake. They think they know best how to handle certain topics. Pride may even convince them that their misappropriation of truth is proof that they are actually more devoted to Christ than others. Like Peter, if they follow their story long enough, they will grow only more and more distant until any affiliation with Christ or biblical Christianity is unrecognizable.

Others make the mistake I did that day on the interstate. They fail to recognize just how important it is to close the gap. Apathy is a killer in any relationship, and our bond with Christ is no different. One day without alone time with God becomes two, then becomes a week, then months. One semester without joining a small group becomes years without discipleship. The next thing you know, you're way outside the Christian "city limits" and wondering how you got there.

I guess I could have blamed our dilemma on the evening traffic around Mobile. There were thousands of cars on the road, and I've already mentioned how many trucks there were. In all that confusion it's difficult to tell one from the other. The same is true in our lives. We are constantly bombarded with other voices telling us how to live. Every time we open social media or turn on the TV, another truck pulls into the lanes of our lives. Many look a lot like what we've already been following.

So many Christians have been affected by voices that, from the right distance, seem to align with values espoused by Christianity. Podcasters, speakers, and online influencers have gained followings in the church, often to the detriment of Christian listeners because, while they may have some trappings of Christian thought, at their foundation they are not heading in the same direction as the kingdom. The only way for a believer to discern the difference is to follow Christ closely. When you invest time in the Word and walk in the Holy Spirit, you will not be easily led astray by the traffic of our world.

I cannot tell you how many times I hear Christians having conversations about their courses of action, when the answer has been explicitly given in God's Word. There are some things that don't have to be prayed about, counseled about, or even considered. The Bible is beautifully clear on marriage, sexuality, gender, truth, and many more issues that seem to confound nominal Christians.

When you invest time in the Word and walk in the Holy Spirit, you will not be easily led astray by the traffic of our world.

On most issues you do not have to assume which direction God wants you to take. With the guidance of the Scriptures, prayer, and the counsel of mature believers, you'll find that many things we wrestle with are clear. However, when you have a life without discipleship and without time in God's Word, you're flying blind. You're like me at the end of that exit, choosing which way to turn based on some gut feeling that has little to do with reality.

The only way to avoid guessing your way through the Christian life is to actively engage in following Jesus. The greatest tool you have for that job is the Holy Bible. However, just owning a Bible won't help you navigate life. You have to read it thoughtfully and frequently so your worldview aligns with God's truth. One study by the Center for Bible Engagement showed that the number one predictor of spiritual growth was whether or not the person read the Bible at least four times each week. People who did so were statistically proved to be twice as likely to share their faith, while also seeing incredible reductions in destructive habits like viewing pornography.[1]

We were created to have deep relationship with God. This is evident in the effects of time spent reading and studying Scripture. Not only does this valuable time augment our biblical perspective and draw us closer to God; it also has measurable effects in mental health and well-being.

In stark contrast to the positive effects of time in God's Word, professing believers who are less frequent in their reading show very little difference from unbelievers in both behavior and spiritual health. Reading your Bible once a week will not do it. This lack of biblical understanding is having devastating results on the church, and it is just as devastating for you as an individual Christian. If the majority of your days does not include thoughtful time in the Bible, you are following from a distance.

For Blake and me, our wrong turn could have been more quickly discovered if we had not been so distracted.

We were talking, we were living, we were checking out the building projects along our route. We weren't paying attention to where we were going. When I finally paused to think about our route, I realized we indeed had a problem.

What is distracting you? Those distractions cause us to follow the wrong leaders to the wrong destinations. If we had followed long enough, we would have probably ended up at some confused guy's house, trying to explain why we had followed him. If it had gone on long enough, we may have been explaining to the police why we had followed someone into his driveway. The point is, we would have followed him to his destination, but it would not have been ours.

Too many Christians are following consumerism to debt and a lack of fulfillment. Others are following status to a destination where they may matter for a moment—until the next big thing comes along. Others are driving the dark roads of life as they follow "self" to an undeveloped dead end of no meaningful purpose. Others find themselves walking into a new church or classroom convinced that they have encountered the adventure of new and deeper thinking, only to be led into the destructive dead end of some unscriptural ideology.

What are you following? The only way to know is to take a moment and closely examine where you are, where it seems you're heading, and what or who is leading you there. Does it sound loving but lack convictional truth? Look closer: It may not be Christian at all. Does it invite you to be a strong person but not speak of a relationship with God? Look closer: It may be self-sufficiency, not

Christ-dependence. Is it new and hip but counters clear biblical teaching? Look closer: It may be not revelation but heresy.

On the road that day, I did not realize what was happening until I really started paying attention. Let me challenge you to pay attention to what is happening in your spiritual life. Pay attention to what your favorite speaker is saying and not saying. Pay attention to the trajectory of your faith life. You may just realize that following from a distance is not following Him at all.

CLOSING THE GAP

When I recognized I was off course, I had to do something. Blake and I started googling tire shops and looking for anything that sounded familiar. We started frantically making calls, knowing most tire shops were either closed or about to close. Eventually, we were able to locate the correct tire shop. When we got there, Blake's new tire had already been mounted on the rim and was ready to go, and we all headed back to the interstate. After a few laughs, a hearty thank-you, and paying our kind rescuer, we were finally going home.

The situation would never have been corrected unless we had taken time to stop, identify where we needed to be, and set our course to get there. Likewise, I want to suggest that you take a moment to think about where you are with the Lord. Are you walking closely with Him, hand in hand, trusting Him and His Word for your life? Or are you following at a distance—susceptible to distractions, lame philosophies, and compromises? Wherever you are in your journey, I want you to know that you are the one who dropped back, not God. He is right where He's supposed to be. He loves you and awaits you with open arms. And guess what: You won't need Google to find Him.

Traffic had cleared up by the time we finally headed home. When I got in my truck and followed Blake's taillights into the night, I couldn't help but think, "If only I had just followed more closely."

Scan the QR code or visit bit.ly/4nKK3N3 to stay (Un)Embarrassed and encouraged by subscribing to my YouTube channel.

Chapter 3

THE DEADLY DRIFT

*Examine yourselves to see whether you are in the
faith; test yourselves. Do you not realize that Christ
Jesus is in you—unless, of course, you fail the test?*
—2 Corinthians 13:5

Michael was in my youth group. Little by little, he found a way to explain away all the commands and guidance of Scripture. Today, he is angry with evangelical Christians and fully engaged in an LGBTQ-affirming apostate "church."

Anna was a pastor's kid we knew for years. At a nominally Christian university, she fell under the influence of progressive professors. Today, she is married to another woman.

Brooke grew up in the same circles I did, both of us being preacher's kids. Not long ago I heard she is an atheist, angry at a God she denies and at His church.

Gabe was super talented, a real leader and influencer

in every circle, with a bright future in the ministry. Today, after several scandals instigated by his loose grasp on Scripture, he is a "spiritual" social media influencer, teaching an empty, humanist perversion of the gospel.

You probably have some stories just like mine, tragic tales of friends you witnessed abandoning the faith. Some have gone so far as to become hostile to anything resembling Christian orthodoxy. You know the heartbreak of watching a formerly faithful brother or sister become a reliable voice for the positions most contrary to views you once shared.

The stories that open this chapter are personal for me, full of the painful reality that accompanies someone close to you being pulled toward destruction. I have seen it too many times among friends and colleagues. I have seen it happen to people within my own church family. I've watched as they allowed themselves to be influenced by the treacherous whisper of worldly wisdom and to deconstruct, only to be reassembled as salespeople of Satan's lying refrain: "Did God really say...?" (Gen. 3:1).

There is a spiritual and intellectual contagion in the church. We have been infected by the disease of humanistic hubris carrying with it a gospel based on the goodness of man and rejection of any need for repentance. The sexual and gender confusion gods of this age have intertwined choice with identity, leading pulpits to offer "ministry" that dulls the senses and despises anything so judgmental as being delivered, changed, or born again as a new creature in Christ. A false enlightenment is occurring, whereby age-old truth is laid aside in the name of fresh understanding and creative, feelings-based herme-neutics. As academics, influencers, and pastors are themselves infected, this deadly epidemic is laying exponential waste to churches, families, and individuals.

It doesn't have to be like this. There is no reason for the church or for you as a believer to accept that seeing our friends and family apostatize is just some sort of new normal. Yes, the Scriptures warn of a great "falling away" (2 Thess. 2:3, NKJV). The Word also teaches that the Spirit of God will pour out on sons and daughters. Many will abandon the faith, but the people you care about do not have to be counted among those who lose their way. Neither do you.

The drift into losing one's faith or finding a soul-destroying replacement for one's faith is not a foregone conclusion. However, to be prevented, it must be understood. We must grasp what is happening to the drifting soul. How does a person go from being close to God, walking in relationship with their Creator, to becoming so confused and turned around?

Peter's journey from "I'll die for You" to "I do not know the man" was not an instantaneous junket. Although many preachers and teachers, myself included, have made a quick jump from Peter's former statement to the latter, his descent from devotion to denial unfolded over a series of decisions that left him in a position he never anticipated. The shocking nature of change in Peter and in the deconstructing people we know leads us to believe this must be a complex process. It is actually quite uncomplicated. It starts with just one step away from Jesus.

When we see our friends, family, and old college roommates living in the quagmire of wrong thinking, we tend to make assumptions about how they arrived at that position. We attempt to surmise their motives or offer explanation. It is important to remember that the rationale for abandoning the faith can be as varied as the backgrounds, experiences, and personalities of the individuals. Church hurt, lack of doctrinal grounding, or straightforward immoral proclivities are a few among the plethora of rationales used to explain their ideological straying. The simple truth is, no matter the reasons, every person who winds up lost and wandering started by going just one step off course.

Long before my son, Blake, was the Mustang-driving, standout goalie featured in the last chapter, he had a day that provides a fitting metaphor for the spiritual drift we see around us. We lived in Miami at the time, and he was about six years old. It was a Saturday. My wife, Kelly, was at a women's conference, and I had taken Blake and his sisters to the mall. Outnumbered three to one, I called in reinforcements, and my parents joined us for the day of fun. The kids were having a great time hanging out with their grandparents. We shopped at a few of the big anchor stores and checked out the various goods being touted by vendors throughout the concourses.

"How 'bout some ice cream?"

It was probably my dad who suggested it, and ice cream is always a great idea to kids. My favorite place in the Miami area (Homestead) was La Michoacana, which served incredible, homemade, authentic Mexican ice cream treats. I was ready to head to the car and drive over there, but the kids were already headed toward the mall's ice cream shop. My personal preference would have to wait.

Standing at the counter, I reflected on how blessed I was. To have my kids and parents together, just hanging out on a Saturday, was a dream. My dad was my hero. Seeing him and Mom with the kids was as much a cause for gratitude as any of the success we were seeing in our growing church.

It was my turn to order. The girls had already put their orders in.

"I'll take the mint chocolate chip," I said, then turned to Blake. I didn't spot him.

I quickly scanned my surroundings, thinking maybe he was grabbing some napkins, climbing under a nearby table, or finding a seat on one of the benches in the middle of the mall. But I didn't see him anywhere. Everyone else—the girls and grandparents—was still there, so no one had taken him to a restroom.

"Mom, have you seen Blake?" Mom shook her head and turned around to look behind her.

A moment ago, he had been there. He was so close when we were waiting to place our orders that I had physically bumped into him. Now he was nowhere to be seen. Someone quickly checked to make sure he had not gone to the nearby restroom, then we spread out to look for him. Nothing. My son was lost.

If you have ever had one of those moments when you think you've lost your child or they've wandered off, you know what I was feeling. There is an adrenaline rush as a frantic search begins. Usually, you find them playing quietly in a room you had not thought to check or out in the neighbor's backyard checking out a new puppy. It's a terrible feeling fortunately cut short by the quick discovery that all is well.

On this day, I hoped for that moment. But no matter how hard I tried, I could not will it into existence. I stared into the moving crowd, imagining that if I just looked a little harder, I would spot him, as if my gaze somehow could make a boy materialize. The adrenaline rush became a sinking, slow churn in my stomach. A deluge of what-ifs bombarded my thoughts.

What if this were one of the real ones? What if someone took my boy? What if he wandered out of the mall and into traffic? What if he was hurt somewhere? What if we could not find him? There was also a really big question: What would I tell his mom?

What felt like an eternity but was only a few minutes passed quickly. I knew we needed help if we were going to find him. Seeing a nearby security guard, I told him what was happening. His impassive reaction told me he was quite accustomed to situations like this. We went through a few questions and rechecked a few obvious places as the mood quickly became more serious.

A few more security guards showed up. They spread the word that a child had been separated from his parents. Blake's description was sent out over their radios. Our family spread out, searching for him as best we could while one of us stayed close to security in case they heard something. They informed us that all store managers and kiosk operators had been notified. Surely, someone would see him soon.

Miami is incredibly diverse. There were over sixty nationalities represented in the congregation of the church I led. The predominant shades of hair and skin tone were darker than any in our family. Making the contrast even more stark was the presence of many Central and South Americans who would travel to Miami for shopping. Dolphin Mall's proximity to the airport made it a prime destination for those tourists. Just as when Kourtney decided to separate herself from Dad on the way into her school, it was usually effortless to spot a Johnson kid among a crowd. Having kids with light hair always made it easier to find them. Today was no different. I imagined that would have to help.

I was right. We may have spent a little more on childhood sunscreen during those Miami summers, but on this day, Blake's fair hair and light skin paid off. Shop owners and mall employees reported seeing the little blond kid being carried along by the current of the crowd. But there was one problem: Blake had been taught not to talk to strangers.

Word began to trickle back that he'd been spotted, but nobody could stop him. Every time someone would try to call out to him or get close to him, he would avoid them and disappear back into the crowd. Each report came from farther and farther away. In his confusion, Blake was denying the very help that could have ended this terrible ordeal. He was now actively running from rescue.

Eventually, a security employee managed to corral Blake and bring him back to us. Relieved is an understatement of my feelings the moment I saw my little buddy. Many hugs followed.

"Dad, all these people were trying to catch me," Blake said, oblivious to the precarious nature of the situation.

Not wanting him or the girls to know just how bad things could have been, I could only whisper a prayer of gratitude. Thank God my little boy was back.

We would talk about that day many times over the ensuing years, sometimes as one of those inside jokes all families have, but always with the grateful understanding that it could have turned out much differently. I have often thought about what it must have been like to be Blake on that day, to have been the kid aimlessly drifting farther and farther away from his family.

How did it happen? What was it like? How did he end up so far from us so quickly?

ONE STEP AWAY

Once again, the answer to how it all began is a simple one. Blake got distracted by something. He may have been looking at all the ice cream flavors. Maybe he was watching a toy he longed for pass by under the arm of a nearby child. Or he may have been fighting imaginary space invaders that had infiltrated the shopping center. I don't know what caused him to start the drift, but I know his being lost started with just one step away from us. Then another, and another.

This was the window of opportunity that could have

prevented all that followed. If I had seen him drifting away, if he had noticed the distance, or if one of his sisters had turned to catch a glimpse before he rounded the nearest corner, the trauma could have been resolved so quickly. None of that happened. Blake did not notice, and neither did we.

So it is with the vacillating believer. Those first steps of drift are subtle but critical.

As followers of Jesus Christ, we must be honest with ourselves about our walk with God. Paul wrote, "Examine yourselves to see whether you are in the faith; test yourselves" (2 Cor. 13:5). How frequently do we follow this instruction?

We can talk casually about what may have distracted a child at a mall ice cream stand, but the propensity to be distracted is not something that disappears with age. Have you ever neared the end of a week and realized you had not spent much time with God? The first time it happens, it may be obvious (and embarrassing) to you. But after

Those first steps of drift are subtle but critical.

a few weeks like that, you may not recognize it at all. The next thing you know, you'll be drifting along with the crowd—a crowd of popular ideas dissonant to what you've learned to-date about the Christian faith.

Blake may have been distracted by peering over the edge of the counter to see all the possible ice cream flavors and toppings. For many, that's illustrative of how spiritual drift begins. They get distracted by the good things their heavenly Father is bringing into their lives. It seems counterintuitive to be distracted by blessings, but a packed schedule, an unhealthy work-life balance, and even success in our endeavors can all initiate a drift from God's side.

Christians will pray and ask others to join them in prayer about starting a new business, educational journey, relationship, or even ministry. Then when the wheels begin to turn and we see progress, our time in prayer dwindles. We needed God to bless the idea, but now we just need books, advice, or our own effort in order to make progress. We find ourselves blessed by God's hand but no longer making time to be in His presence.

The pattern plays out with disturbing familiarity. A young person is raised in the church, attends youth groups and camps, and serves on teams. Then high school graduation appears on the horizon. They start sending out applications. They ask their youth leaders, pastors, and friends to pray that they are accepted by their top schools. They say, and even sincerely mean the words, that they want to end up exactly where God wants them to be. Then the acceptance letter comes, moving day follows, and they find themselves in a whole new world. Throwing themselves into the studies and social life of college, their Bibles get lost beneath dorm beds, their schedules get too full to find a church, and their hearts begin to drift from God. Cynical professors push them along. By Christmas they are cold, and by the next semester they have turned against everything they thought they believed. They return to their families as hostile strangers, ready to attack the very foundations that got them where they are. Sadly, it all started with being distracted by a good thing.

You've probably seen this in the life of someone you know. It may have even happened to you. It might be happening right now. The new relationship, the new job, the new business, or whatever other good thing becomes a distraction, and the deadly drift has begun.

In that mall there was a multitude of opportunities for Blake to be distracted. The sights, sounds, and environment were created for just that purpose. Every store advertisement, every vendor's voice, and even the building's layout all worked in concert to distract from the world outside, from the bills and responsibilities that waited in the parking lot. They beckoned the shopper: Just buy this. Just sign up for that. Just try one sample, and your life will be improved. Do not miss out—it will be gone tomorrow. One weekend only! Come on in; you have time. Oh, wait, buy some jewelry before you go there. Here's a hot soft pretzel. You need some time in the arcade. Whoa, how have you ever lived without a personal foot-massaging tub? Did you register to win the new Jeep?

Distractions everywhere.

Malls are not what they used to be. In many towns they are barely hanging on or already closed, but the art of diversion is not gone from our lives. Your life is filled with things that exist almost entirely to distract and pull you into their ecosystem. Our devices are some of the worst perpetrators. You may even be reading this book on a device that also sends notifications from a litany of apps that profit by grabbing your attention. Scrolling through feeds, binge-watching the latest streaming hit, going on YouTube rabbit-hole journeys, or scanning the latest headlines can all distract us from taking time for the spiritual...and we wind up like a lost kid at the mall.

FROM DISTRACTION TO DESTRUCTION

When a person drifts spiritually, they eventually take a wrong turn. As we spend less time with God, we become less like Him and more like the world around us. Our sense of spiritual discernment weakens, and our moral compass goes askew. It's just a matter of time before we wind up making some sinful or destructive decision. Satan loves this moment.

Sin separates us from God. Sin pushes God's Word from our lives. Earlier, we learned about the importance of daily Bible reading. There is an old saying that your Bible will keep you from sin or your sin will keep you from the Bible. As paradoxical as it is to run from the very thing that will bring us life, the first human reaction to sin is to distance ourselves from God. It has been true since Adam and Eve fled into the bushes at the sound of His voice.

The distance of drifting increases as sin enters the story. When we begin to hide from God and other believers, we find ourselves wandering further and further. Just like Blake becoming more and more disoriented, the drifter finds that going from distracted to distant to hopelessly lost happens faster than imagined.

This is when you begin to see formerly faithful believers take positions contrary to God's Word. If it seems that the drift from Spirit-filled youth group to full-on "progressive" and unscriptural ideology happens fast, it is because it happens while we're not paying attention. Like sleeping in a canoe upstream of a waterfall, it starts simply but gains speed quickly. Drift is real, and drift can be deadly.

The it-could-have-been-worse thoughts about that day at the mall abound. A child wandering a mall in a major city is no small thing. There is a laundry list of potentially bad outcomes that could come from such a situation. Things turned out well only because of God's grace and the actions of a network of people: our family, mall security, and other mall employees.

Navigating the pitfalls of a sin-sick world is as dangerous to our souls as Blake walking through that mall. It matters whom we travel with. If Blake had been traveling alone, no one would have known he was missing. Other shoppers would have given little notice to the boy in the crowd. If they noticed him at all, they would have assumed he had friends or family nearby. The only ones who knew he was out of place were his family, the people traveling with him.

Isolation kills. It's difficult to realize we are drifting spiritually when we don't have a steady fellowship on whom we can rely. We need faithful, truth-telling people around us, whether it be family, close friends, or a small group. Better yet, we need all those. Someone must be able to tell us when our moods are off, when our responses seem different, or when we're growing spiritually apathetic or withdrawn.

It is not enough to be around a lot of people. Blake was in the middle of a crowded mall, but that did him precious little good. In life it's not enough to have a robust list of social events or interactions. We need fellow believers who are journeying with us. Having a life full of people is not the same as having Christ-devoted friends who can recognize when we drift—and who have the courage (and our blessing) to point out what's happening. If you do not have any of those relationships, start them now. Seek out fellow believers to befriend. Plug into a local congregation, or find a small group at your church. Do not travel alone.

In a world of kid-tracking smartwatches, we could have found Blake a bit more quickly. We could have possibly called him and learned where he was. But that technology had not caught on yet, so we had to intercede for help on his behalf. Likewise, it's not enough to have people in our lives who can sound the alarm when we begin to drift. We also need people who can intercede for us in prayer.

Who is praying for you? No, really, whom are you communicating with about the needs and dangers in your life?

On the other hand, are you an intercessor? When you see someone drifting, do you talk about them to others, or do you engage in prayer for their endangered soul? Every believer should have people in their life who pray for them and people for whom they pray. Without intercession Blake's story would have been different. Without spiritual intercession the drifters in our lives are doomed.

Again, Peter's journey from "I'll die for You" to "I do not know the man" started with just one step away from Jesus. He had failed to stand alongside his Master as He was bound and taken away from Gethsemane. Fearfully, Peter followed from a distance.

~

And now, he sat in the dirt, leaning back against the cool wall of a house, staring blankly through red-rimmed eyes, sweat and tears leaving salty trails down his face. As his bitter tears of shame were soaked up by the ground, he wished the ground would swallow him up too. He had no memory of ever weeping like this before, ever feeling like this before. He was a tough guy, a commercial fisherman, a man's man. Crying alone in a Jerusalem alley was not something he could have imagined himself doing. But here he was.

"It was that wretched bird," he thought to himself.

Why did the rooster have to crow? Why not just skip that infernal racket for one morning? The foul creature. He would wring its neck if he could find it.

No, the rooster was not the wretch. Peter was. The memory of making eye contact with Jesus caused a hot groundswell of new tears. It was a wonder he had any tears left, but somehow a fresh flow flooded into his swollen eyes and down his cheeks. With a guttural moan, Peter slumped to his side, the acrid tears making fresh rivulets in the dust.

It was more than the look, the adrenaline rush of the moment in the garden, and even the fact that he had almost been caught in his lies by those in the courtyard. Something else gnawed at him. Jesus always had this way of looking at him or through him when He spoke. It was His words earlier, in the Upper Room, that haunted Peter now.

Jesus had known this would happen. He had looked Peter in the eye, regarded him with loving sorrow, and told him this moment was coming—denial before the rooster crowed. He even said He had prayed for Peter. And there was something else.

"Peter, when you have turned again, strengthen your brothers."

What did Jesus mean by "strengthen your brothers"? Why did it even matter now? Jesus had been arrested and beaten. Peter had failed to stand up for Him—failed to stop the atrocity, failed to even be brave enough to die alongside his teacher. What was the purpose of even thinking about strengthening his brothers now?

∼

Eventually, Peter would discover the answer to his questions. Meanwhile, he sat somewhere in the Holy City grieving over his failures. However, he was not the only one who should be puzzled by the statement Jesus made. There was something in His words that is very telling for the rest of us.

Jesus knew that, on the other side of failure, Peter's best moment was coming. He knew Peter would weep bitterly, but He also knew that when the Holy Spirit would be poured out on His followers, Peter would deliver a Pentecost sermon that would be foundational for the church. The people who were converted after Peter's message would be the first wave of believers carrying the gospel throughout the known world. Peter was destined to be a leader. He was undoubtedly a man of influence.

We all know people like Peter. They have contagious passion and can effortlessly turn a dull moment into a lively one, sway an entire audience through an impassioned speech, and inspire action in the most reluctant of people. They are doers; their followers fall in line based on some unexplainable magnetism. They are influencers, not in the mere modern context of social media but in a manner that transcends all communication and connections. Peter was an influencer. Jesus knew this and, in that exchange, He was calling forth Peter's power to lead and influence others.

Perhaps that is what provoked the sifting; Satan wanted to destroy Peter because he knew the fiery disciple was a danger to the kingdom of hell. In just a few days a group of disciples would follow Peter on a fishing excursion; within months he would be a leader of the church. Satan and Jesus were both cognizant of the impact Peter could have on his fellow disciples and on others. Whether that influence resulted in good or evil was subject to the path Peter chose. Whatever the path, others were sure to follow.

You may not see yourself as that influential. When you look within the church and see the popular speakers and talented worship leaders, you probably think they're the ones who can really influence others. You're not wrong. Those who hold various positions in the church are influential. Their actions can hold incredible sway over other

Christians. This is why the Bible offers such explicit warnings about the conduct of church leaders, especially those who teach doctrine to others. With their influence comes heavy responsibility to honor the Lord and get it right, for they will be judged by God regarding how they handle it.

THE POWER AND PERIL OF INFLUENCE

Two of the stories you've already read in this book are about my son being lost. In one he was lost while riding in the truck with me. In the other he was lost while we were at the mall. Both stories included Blake and me. Each time, I was the responsible party—his father. But my role was different in each event.

When we were at the mall, I had a responsibility to care for Blake, to guide him, to protect him, and to provide for his needs throughout the day. When I discovered he had drifted outside my protection, I immediately engaged in my obligation to find him. I searched for him. I called his name. I interceded for help in locating him. He was lost, and I helped find him.

On the evening we got lost trying to follow the good Samaritan to a tire repair shop, our roles were similar, but my responsibility was different. That night, Blake didn't wander away. He was not distracted by something passing by. He did not take steps to distance himself from where he was supposed to be. On that night, Blake sat in my truck and trusted me to get him where he needed to go. Yet he ended up lost.

Both nights saw Blake get lost, once because he drifted

and once because he trusted someone who was following from a distance. That night, I did not follow closely enough. I got distracted by our conversation and allowed the distance between me and the truck I followed to trick me into following a similar truck in the wrong direction. I made the decisions and took every turn. All Blake did was ride along with Dad; when Dad got lost, so did he.

Those who lead in the church, those who help others find their way as they attempt to follow Jesus, are like me in the driver's seat. Blake jumped into my truck and trusted me. People seek out churches, join small groups, follow Bible teachers, and enroll in seminaries fully expecting that they can trust those who will guide their journey. In a sense, they are just along for the ride. Unfortunately, not all their teachers are following Jesus.

Paul told the Corinthians, "Follow my example, as I follow the example of Christ" (1 Cor. 11:1). His word *follow* can be translated to "imitate"—imitate him as he imitates Christ. That's a pretty safe way to live life, if the one you imitate is the apostle Paul. However, Paul is not around these days, so you should be extremely careful whom you follow.

> *Discernment is knowing the difference not between right and wrong but between right and almost right.*

Charles Spurgeon, the acclaimed pastor often referred to as the prince of preachers, once said that discernment is knowing the difference not between right and wrong but between right and almost right. As the world grows more confusing and absolute truth is valued less than ever, Spurgeon's words ring even truer. So many of the wicked ideologies being fed to Christians today have a hint of truth but are toxic to the soul. The false teachers and purveyors of the perversion known as progressive Christianity are quite skilled in doling out conveniently improvised doctrines that have the essence of almost right while being absolutely wrong.

There are few things more heartbreaking than a family raising their child in the faith, instructing them in the things of God, and keeping them involved in church groups and activities, only to lose them when they go off to college. This terrible reality is all the more agonizing when the chosen institution was one recommended by their church or by Christian acquaintances. Yet this scenario happens every year across almost every denomination and Christian movement.

Parents send off a Jesus-loving, respectable young disciple to complete their education. A few semesters later their beloved child is espousing LGBTQ ideology and twisting Scripture to do so. Their child, who was dedicated in the name of the Father, Son, and Holy Spirit, comes back for spring break telling Mom and Dad that God is a gender-fluid, sex-positive force for good in the world. Parents who labor for years to build a small business find themselves rebuked by a suddenly ungrateful child who wants them to know that Jesus is a Marxist and that they are an oppressive class of greedy capitalists. Imagine the parents' surprise when they find out these lies were being fed to them not by some roommate, fellow student, or university free-speech activists but by professors at a so-called Christian university!

There is a heavy reckoning ahead for those who have infiltrated Christian academia with their pseudo-intellectual, liberally enlightened doctrines. Entire generations of good young people are being destroyed by academics who are more concerned with the latest educational theories, academia trends, and creative hermeneutics than they are with the souls of the young people entrusted to their leadership. Even heavier judgment is coming for those who have allowed these wolves in among the sheep in the name of social acceptance and ecumenical inclusivity.

Christians must be increasingly vigilant regarding who is allowed to influence and educate their children. When young people sit in a classroom with a heretic who pushes falsehood or with scoffers who think they know better than God's Word, they could end up far from where we hoped they would be.

While there is much discussion to be had regarding the dangerous influences residing in institutions of higher education, the most egregious perpetrators of evil influence are found closer to home. Far too many pulpits have been filled by weak, cowardly, unspiritual, and unscriptural "pastors" who lead people astray through a myriad of false teachings. Entire books have been written about individual heresies and deceptions, and I won't take time to discuss them all. However, a few converge in a mendacious witch's brew of toxic thought, and I would be remiss if I didn't take a moment to expose them.

The first ingredient in the poison being distributed to

the saints is the prioritization of feelings. By *feelings* I'm not referring to the emotional response that occurs by way of an experience with the presence and power of the Holy Spirit in a worship environment. That is a very real part of our faith. However, there is danger in becoming a church that emphasizes creating a space for an emotional experience over making room for people to have a real encounter with God. A church that consistently minimizes or avoids the preaching of the gospel, including the confrontation of sin, is doing nothing to save and strengthen the souls of the people who gather.

If times of corporate worship are not accompanied by sound doctrine, we should not be surprised when people apostatize despite regular participation in our worship services. Without sound preaching and teaching of the Word, without uncompromising truth being regularly poured into the people, they will be easily influenced by the false winds and empty clouds of this world's anti-God philosophies. When someone leaves the church fellowship to pursue a sinful lifestyle because they "feel" that is who they really are, churches should not be surprised—this person was already following their feelings, and not Jesus, far before walking out the door.

Feelings being the most important consideration of the preacher or church leadership has led many churches to completely abandon anything that looks like a call to repentance and forgiveness. How could they possibly do something so mean as to call someone to change or reject their grievous choices? So they say nothing that could hurt anyone or even make them uncomfortable. Instead of calling people to a life-changing, soul-saving encounter with Jesus, these pulpits spoon out a lukewarm porridge of self-discovery and motivation. The only person these churches risk offending is God.

When feelings have taken center stage in the church, the next ingredient follows naturally: personal interpretation of Scripture. Fewer and fewer are the churches that approach Scripture with the understanding that a God-devoted writer, inspired and guided by the Holy Spirit, wrote something that he meant to say in a particular way to a particular audience—invoking principles of absolute truth to be applied to the life of any believer who would later encounter the writing. But today liberal teachers and preachers encourage believers to interpret biblical texts through their own personal lenses.

If you are a feminist, the Scriptures become feminist. If you are a liberation theologian, then a passage is to be read in that light. If you are a nonbinary furry, then the Scripture must be viewed from that extremely unscriptural perspective. Why not? The moment we decided that every person gets to apply their own secular worldview to Scripture, instead of weighing their worldview against the absolute truth of Scripture, all boundaries were eliminated. No longer do we ask what Scripture says. Now all that matters is "what it means to me."

The danger contained in this mixture of feelings-first and personalized hermeneutics cannot be overstated. When the church rounds off the edges of the gospel, we're left with an empty shell of a belief system that can do nothing to save the souls or enrich the lives of those who follow after it. Instead of being salt and light, churches have been reduced to church lite, carrying some of the flavors but none of the substance of a biblical fellowship. When the pulpit operates in fear of causing offense, it loses the very essence of a gospel that both confronts death-bringing sin and offers lifesaving change. What remains is an antigospel that soothes the feelings and numbs the conscience while leaving souls hopelessly trapped. This quite literally denies the power of God's truth and destroys countless lives.

The pastors and churches that have fallen into this mire have little answer for the gods of the age—particularly the world's obsession with sexual identity as the central human characteristic. The world says, "If you deny my right to have sexual experiences in any way I see fit," or, "If you do not accept that I can identify myself by any number of nonsensical genders or species," then "You are denying my existence." In reality it's quite absurd to say that if we reject the idea of a man pretending he is an antelope or a woman having the right to marry a panda, we reject their human existence. It is equally absurd to contend that when we say sex was created by a loving God for monogamous, married, heterosexual couples, we deny the very being of those wanting to be freed from natural norms they consider restrictive. That is what they tell us: "Unless you agree with me, you are denying my truth or attempting to erase me."

Tolerance is not enough in today's culture. Christians are no longer allowed to simply go about their lives and accept that not all their neighbors share their moral views. Now business owners are expected to fly the right flag during the right month—or face boycott. Churches are expected to be silent on issues of sexuality. Christian parents are scorned if they dare question pornographic material being offered in their children's library. Sexual proclivity has become so intertwined with human essence that to question a person's choices is deemed an attack on their right to exist. This has ended almost all discourse on the subject, as any dissension from radical ideology is anathema and grounds for social cancellation.

When feelings are paramount and Scripture is deemed relative, weakened churches are increasingly susceptible to the prevailing ideology of the day. Once-stalwart denominations now march under the LGBTQ banner. Entire movements have split over whether they would be gay-affirming—including the ordination of homosexual and transgender clergy. Even within denominations that have remained faithful, growing numbers of influencers are signaling support for popular, sinful lifestyles while others, including leaders, are frozen in place by their own obsession with being likable and inoffensive.

ONE STANDARD

It was never God's intention for the pulpit to be led by the pew. Those who lead or teach in the church are to have one standard of truth: God's Word. The apostle Paul clearly warned us, "The time will come when people will not put up with sound doctrine. Instead, to suit their own desires, they will gather around them a great number of teachers to say what their itching ears want to hear" (2 Tim. 4:3).

Unfortunately, the evidence clearly shows that we have arrived at that moment.

Now we are left with precious little when it comes to voices for righteousness. Anything deemed controversial is avoided, no matter what the Bible teaches on the subject. Too many pastors, more concerned with their positions than with truth, are leading people to hell while withholding the cure for what ails them. Too many organizations and denominations, more concerned with their coffers and footprints, have done little to correct those within their ranks who are in error, even those who blatantly support wickedness.

Parents must not take a back seat in their children's lives and just drift along.

James wrote, "Not many of you should become teachers, my fellow believers, because you know that we who teach will be judged more strictly" (3:1). Every church leader and teacher, every Christian speaker or author, and leaders of every denomination or Christian organization should revisit this verse and what it means. Like my night on the interstate, when you invite people to ride with you, you bear great responsibility. If they end up off course, they will suffer, and you will be judged for taking them there.

The responsibility for guiding others is not unique to pastors and teachers. While churches are being pulled down by pew-directed pastors, many lives are being destroyed by child-led parents. Parents must remember they are called to raise their children, not befriend them. There will be times when being a proactive parent will create animosity in children. If Mom and Dad are patient and stay the course, they'll find that the hard feelings are temporary. Despite what children may say when trying to get their way, children and teenagers want parents to take an active, intentional, and, yes, disciplinary role in their lives. They have an innate understanding that these actions are proof their parents love them.

Parents cannot get distracted from being active in the lives of their children. While every home may have different parameters for choosing friends, for deciding at what age sleepovers are appropriate, or for when children should have access to smartphones and the internet, there must be parameters of some sort. Christian parents should be rooted in biblical principles and guided by spiritual discernment. Parents must not take a back seat in their children's lives and just drift along. We must be prayerfully, lovingly active in the everyday moments of their lives.

I made my first mistake on the interstate that night by not following closely enough the moment we pulled out onto the road. I should have been right on that truck's bumper. Spiritually, parents should remember that it is very hard for children to be closer to God, to be more interested in spiritual things, than their parents are. If you are concerned about your children having a relationship with God, make sure *you* model the joy, blessings, and disciplines of following Christ.

How do your children think you feel about church attendance? Do you find excuses to miss church activities, or are they central to your family calendar? Do your kids see you spending time on social media but not enjoying God's Word personally? What in your life illustrates for them what abundant life in Christ is all about?

They are watching. Not only do they hear what you say; they are watching what you do. When you make an off-color comment or get enraged in traffic, they are watching. When you are hypocritical, you teach them that it's OK to be hypocritical. Or worse, you may be teaching them that everyone is a hypocrite—so what's the point of being a Christian at all?

Parents, leaders, pastors, academics, and anyone else responsible for guiding people in their walk with God all have an awesome responsibility to live out their duty prayerfully. And if you aren't in one of those roles, you're not free of obligation. You are influencing someone. It could be a coworker, a friend, or even your spouse, but every person's actions have the potential to influence others. All of us who call ourselves Christian must be careful to think, speak, and act like one.

How many people have been led astray because Christians in their lives influenced them away from God? It could be through venting church hurt, through gossip, or through giving advice from a popular perspective rather than God's Word. The saddest reality is when the person responsible for leading someone astray finally gets their own struggles sorted out. They get over the hurt, find out their gossip was false, or come to a biblical understanding of the issue they'd gotten wrong, but they are never able to go back and fix the damage they caused in the life of another.

Every one of us has a choice in how we follow Jesus. We are either at His side, pursuing Him with all our might, or, like Peter, following from a distance. When we begin to think of how each one of us is an influencer, we come to recognize that we are indeed exerting a pull on others. Are we pulling people closer to God or further away?

Jesus told Peter that he would become an influence for good and would strengthen his brothers. Just as there is great risk in leading others to wrong destinations, there is also great reward in leading them on the right path. In fact, bold faith, uncompromising truth, and refusal to do anything other than pursue God wholeheartedly have a way of drawing people to Him, not away from Him.

When I was faced with people attending my church who told me they planned to enter a homosexual marriage, I had a choice. I could have determined that their feelings were the most important thing in the conversation. I could have allowed them to have their own personal view of what the Bible says about marriage. I could have decided that any resistance to their decision would be considered an erasure of them as humans and simply said nothing. I could have done a lot of things, but there was only one right response. I had to look them in the eye and tell them what the Word of God says. I let them know that God loves them and I love them—but that God and I do not endorse their decision.

Seeing the influence of the world's view in my church, I had to stand in the pulpit and declare that our church is one where every person is welcome but that sin is something to be set free from. I let them know that we love every person, and because we do, they can expect to hear unfiltered truth from our pulpit. Contrary to what some would assume, these bold actions did not hurt our church. We did not see a mass exodus of people who wanted to get away from "mean-spirited rhetoric" or "hateful bigotry." Instead, our church grew. We saw hundreds of people flock to our services, eager to hear the gospel, experience a life-changing encounter with Jesus, and be discipled as His faithful followers.

Bold faith works for churches, and it works for individual relationships. Our friends who planned to enter a marriage we opposed did not become our enemies. They remained our friends; we were able to minister to them in the future. We remained a light in their lives because they knew we loved them enough to tell them hard truth—that we believed the Bible always, not just when convenient.

Charlotte had been in a same-sex relationship with another woman for some time. She came to church and met Jesus. Immediately, her life started to change, and she wanted to be baptized. I knew Charlotte was at a precarious moment in her faith and that she had not left the relationship she was in. Financially, she didn't think she could make it on her own, so she was trying to work out how to follow Jesus and stay with her girlfriend. I told her I could not baptize her while she was living in that relationship. I could have lowered the bar, put her feelings first, and acted in what some would errantly call "love." Instead, I stayed true to God's way. Today, Charlotte is married to a man, and together they have a beautifully biblical household. That is what happens when we recognize the power of the influence we have and when we use it while staying true to Christ.

The beautiful reality is that influence can be used for good, even if you have not always done so. During a Jesus Revolution moment in our church, a young man named Dallas came to know Jesus. He has a personality that attracts and influences. Before accepting Christ as his Savior, Dallas had lived the fast life of a young man who did not know God at all. Since then, I cannot remember the last time we held a baptism service that did not include someone Dallas had led to Jesus or someone he once sold weed too. Many of them were in both categories.

The incredible story of Dallas's influence can be yours. You are influencing someone every single day. In some sense every person who reads this book has someone following them. The question is, In what direction are you leading?

Scan the QR code or visit bit.ly/ 4gSjlPW to check out these two great moments: when I hired Dallas Davis as my young adults pastor and when Junior Muhubao stood with me, preaching to thirty thousand people in front of the People's Palace in the Democratic Republic of the Congo.

PART II

DENIAL AND DECONSTRUCTION

Chapter 4

THE DECONSTRUCTION OF SIMON PETER

A servant girl noticed him in the firelight and
began staring at him. Finally she said, "This man
was one of Jesus' followers!" But Peter denied it.
"Woman," he said, "I don't even know him!"

—Luke 22:56–57, NLT

I F YOU FOLLOW any of my social media, you have probably encountered Amie (not her real name) in the comments. She loves to show up whenever I make a post that
touches on any of the controversial issues of the day, particularly those regarding gender and sexual ideology.
Typically, she will drop into those conversations for the
purpose of lecturing Christians about how backward,
closed-minded, and unloving we are. In her mind, taking
a bold position against sin simply drives people away

from the gospel, and it is unthinkable to tell people that a new life in Christ calls for living by biblical principles.

Based on her reactions to my posts and anyone who agrees with me, you may think Amie was always a raving leftist, raised by purple-haired, Marxist professors of gender studies at Berkeley. Actually, I have known Amie for many years. We grew up in the same churches, shared mutual friends and acquaintances, and began engaging in ministry around the same time. Somewhere our paths radically diverged, and our similarities became negligible. She is now living in a same-sex relationship while employed as a ministry leader in an apostate church. It is baffling that we ended up in such different places.

When we hear stories like Amie's, we may wonder whether something exists within us that could lead to the same sort of outcome. While we certainly hope we'll never find ourselves literally working in opposition to God's Word, we should be careful never to assume that our own deconstruction is impossible. As Paul warned, "If you think you are standing firm, be careful that you don't fall!" (1 Cor. 10:12). Paul knew that within each believer lie the latent tendencies, characteristics, and past experiences that could pull us toward failure. He was aware of his own weaknesses and wrote about them several times. In his apostolic role providing guidance and oversight to congregations, he had also witnessed the devastating effects after someone in the congregation invited sin into the church. He knew the danger was real, and so should we. We should all heed Paul's advice and recognize that we could be candidates for deconstruction.

The encouraging news is that the potential for failure does not make catastrophe inevitable. None of us has to abandon the faith. We do not have to be swayed by earthly philosophy or by the powers of this world. Our story can be one of overcoming if we do what Paul said: Be careful.

Being careful includes every area of our lives. We should carefully choose what we allow to influence us, what churches we connect to, and with whom we do life. It is also beneficial for us to understand the times and stay aware of the prevailing dangers to ourselves and our families. Most importantly, we should be careful to know ourselves. If you will take time to learn who you are, you can see what motivates you and where you may have weaknesses in character, habits, or experience. Our enemy will capitalize on every deficiency as he assaults your soul.

It is also good to learn from the mistakes and failures of others. We never rejoice when someone falls, nor should we want all the details to satisfy our own morbid curiosity. Nonetheless, we can learn a lot about the tactics of the enemy (and how to overcome them) by considering what happened in the lives of those who have fallen away.

The Bible provides a perfect example of deconstruction in the story of Simon Peter. Although the events unfold over a short period of time, they follow what seems to be a normative arc for those who abandon the faith. Peter even goes so far as to deny knowing Jesus, completing his sad deconstruction narrative.

While the actual collapse of Peter's faith occurs in a relatively short amount of time, we are blessed to have many other areas of Scripture to provide details of who Peter was as a person. Scrutinizing the interactions and activities of the apostle, we find a comprehensive case study of deconstruction not only in his infamous moment of denial but in who he was as a person and how it all came together that fateful night.

Paul was not breaking new ground when he warned against overconfidence in the life of a believer. From childhood he undoubtedly heard and quoted, "Pride goes before destruction, a haughty spirit before a fall" (Prov. 16:18). Peter had probably heard the same wisdom reiterated throughout his own life, but there was a disconnect between what he knew and how he carried himself. Overconfidence seemed to be a theme in the life of the fisherman turned disciple.

You may have a few friends like Peter. Whatever is going on, they are the most committed, at least in the moment. They come with all the energy and swagger of an old pro. These are the five-foot-nine dads carrying late-thirties poundage who swear they could dominate a game of one-on-one with the six-foot-four, two-hundred-pound kid in youth group who's receiving Division 1 scholarship offers. Sometimes it is just lighthearted trash talk, but a fair number of those guys really believe what they're saying.

Peter was probably in earnest when he said he was

ready to go to prison with Jesus—even die for Him. When he contended that his loyalty surpassed that of his fellow disciples, Peter seemed convinced that there was indeed something extraordinary about his level of devotion. He was not like the rest; he would stand when everyone else faltered. When Jesus informed Peter that He had prayed for him, Peter may have thought his Master had wasted His time; Peter's loyalty and strength were not in doubt. Maybe those other guys would fail, but not him!

Hubris led Peter into a dangerous place, and he became self-reliant. He began to overvalue his own ability to withstand difficulty, his wisdom in determining God's will, and the significance of his role in the moment. In the Garden of Gethsemane, he pulled a sword and attempted to alter the course of history. Peter was confident in his ability to be right and to know how that moment should be handled. In his mind, denying Jesus was an absurdity...right up until the moment it happened.

If we're not careful, we will fall into the same trap Peter did, being so convinced of our spiritual strength that we never honestly evaluate our relationship with God.

If we're not careful, we will fall into the same trap Peter did, being so convinced of our spiritual strength that we never honestly evaluate our relationship with God or check our lives for places the enemy is encroaching. Far too many ministries have been cut short, families destroyed, and lives left in ruin because someone thought failure was an impossibility.

As believers it is imperative that we wholeheartedly strive to grow strong spiritually. We must devote quality time to Bible reading and prayer each day, asking the Holy Spirit to guide, guard, and strengthen us. We need to be in small groups. Gathering to worship with like-minded believers is an absolute must. We cannot rest in our own strength or trust our own readiness; we must continue drawing closer to God, growing stronger in Him as long as we live on this earth.

Jay, for example, has struggled with self-confidence for as long as I've known him. From the time he was young, he had a nagging presumption of not being tough enough, good-looking enough, or smart enough to compete with the guys around him. His speech and actions would never have given that away, even to the most attentive observers. He filled conversations with bluster and bravado seasoned by a mix of less-than-good-natured jabs at his cohorts. He worked hard to maintain his image as brave and capable, but a large portion of his efforts was simply a cover for deeply held insecurities. When he revealed to his small group that he had been suicidal and struggled with substance abuse, his friends were shocked because Jay had always seemed on top of the world.

Peter was a lot like Jay. When we watch him wield a sword in the middle of an arrest or throw himself over-board to swim to Jesus and even walk on water, it's easy to see only his confidence. But there was much more to him. On the water when he took his eyes off Jesus, he started to sink. Once the Gethsemane arrest became official, Peter found himself following at a distance—and something began to shift inside him. Maybe his thoughts went to the risk this meant for his family and business. As he saw the growing seriousness of the situation, perhaps he began to fear for his own well-being. We really don't know what went through his mind, but the farther Peter got from Jesus, the more his courage waned.

Even after Pentecost's outpouring of the Holy Spirit and his bold sermon to the masses, Peter seemed to struggle with his own fear. Later, his desire to fit in and preserve his image was so strong that he treated the Gentiles differently depending on who was watching. It was so disturbing to Paul that he not only confronted Peter about it but noted the confrontation in an epistle to the church (Gal. 2:11–12).

All of us have taken a few turns on this seesaw between overconfidence and fear. Within a few minutes, we can go from feeling we could conquer the world to feeling that we are on the cusp of defeat. The truth is, we are not the conquerors; Jesus is. We also have no need to fear defeat because He has overcome the world. The vital balance can be struck only when we arrive at complete reliance on God. Christians who believe themselves invincible will soon find themselves proved wrong; those who think failure is inevitable will soon find themselves proved right. The only antidote to both is full reliance on Christ.

FEAR'S STRANGLEHOLD ON THE CHURCH

If you were to examine the deterioration in the modern church, you would find an abundance of fear. Many pastors are afraid that standing for truth will cost them members and money. Christians in entertainment are afraid that taking a clear stance on the divisive issues of the day will bring on the cancel culture. Parents are afraid that setting clear boundaries will drive their children away. Church leaders and politicians (often eerily similar) operate in obscurity and obfuscation to avoid alienating any pocket of support they need for the next election or appointment.

As fear freezes those responsible for standing against the onslaughts of Satan, the church has lost ground on so many important issues. This pervasive lack of clarity on the part of influencers and leaders is terrible for the church at large. When people read plain truth in the Scriptures but get vague musings from people they expect to help them navigate life, they come to one of two conclusions: Either they misunderstood the Scriptures, or the Scriptures are not all that important. If they did matter, surely those who are biblically educated and supposedly spiritual would be plain about it.

Fear has caused churches to fly the LGBTQ flag over their front doors, lest they be called intolerant. Fear has driven many church leaders to embrace falsehood and support unbiblical ideology, lest they be called bigots. Fear changes the messages in pulpits, the outcomes of church business sessions, and the conversations parents have with their children.

Every time we act in fear, Satan wins. We know that fear is a tool of the enemy and only gives ground to the kingdom of hell. But "God has not given us a spirit of fear, but of power and of love and of a sound mind" (2 Tim. 1:7, NKJV). God has given you and me the power of the indwelling Holy Spirit, a deep love for others that compels us to speak truth, and the soundness of mind to understand His truth. Fear and timidity are not of God. His Holy Spirit empowers us to live in truth—not fooled by the whims of the world or intimidated by the roar of the mob.

Social pressure has a way of affecting us even when it is not as obvious as a mob. Hopefully, you've never experienced one of those social media riots that I've endured a few times. You may not know what it is to have your family members threatened or to be insulted in ways too obscene to publish. Even so, you may have felt pressures in your workplace. You certainly know what it's like to have family or friends contest your biblical view on an issue or situation. You may have even experienced one of those moments when being identified as a faithful Christian could have negative effects on your social standing or career advancement. In those moments what do you do?

Among the many factors assailing Peter that night, he was navigating the social stigma of being the close associate of a condemned man. When you've followed a religious leader and all the established teachers and hierarchy name Him a blasphemous heretic, it's easier if everyone just forgets you know the guy!

Nobody wants to be called hateful, bigoted, racist, misogynistic, or narrow-minded because of what they believe. Satan knows the power of social pressures, and so do those who push wickedness on us. When your life is built around being a person of good character for the glory of God, the last thing you want is for your name to be dragged through the mud. We all know a good name is rather to be chosen than great riches. (See Proverbs 22:1.) Nevertheless, having a good name with God is far more important than having those around you think well of you.

Jesus told us that if we follow Him, the world will hate and persecute us. It makes no sense for the church to expend so much effort attempting to win the approval of people who love what God hates and hate what God loves. If their values are directly opposed to God and they sing your praises, what might that say about you? So do not fall into that trap. You will never please God and be loved by this world.

Peter's self-confidence caused him to misunderstand what God was doing through His Son. Peter's misunderstanding of the unfolding events, and the failure of his own efforts to stop them, fueled the terror within—resulting in his shameful denial. How could someone who spent so much time with Jesus not grasp what was happening? How could someone who had seen Christ come through when human effort failed still respond to adversity through his own strength? How could Peter have been so blind?

We get a window into Peter's cluelessness through something that happened earlier in the night. When we recount the events of that evening, familiar highlights include the last supper, Judas's exit, the arrest, and the trial. But in the middle of those important moments is one less-discussed detail. Between the dinner and the betrayal, Jesus called a prayer meeting in the garden.

Every pastor can relate to Jesus here. Prayer meetings are rarely the most popular gatherings. No one had any trouble showing up for Jesus' thought-provoking teaching. The miraculous healings never failed to draw a crowd, and the loaves and fishes were absolute hits. The prayer meeting was not quite as successful. Very few showed up, and those who did fell asleep within the first hour.

Peter, among others, had received a very specific warning. "Watch and pray so that you will not fall into temptation" (Matt. 26:41) is a compelling piece of guidance when it comes from the Son of God. But Peter and his colleagues were not so impressed. Jesus had hardly disappeared from sight when they fell asleep, leaving Jesus to carry the prayer meeting by Himself.

It's hard to imagine how spiritually dull Peter must have been to sleep in this moment. He had just been told that he would deny Jesus before the rooster crowed. Instead of falling on his face and crying out for help from heaven, he found a comfortable tree to lean against for a nap. What arrogance! What spiritual blindness!

Within the next twelve hours or so, Peter would make the worst mistake of his life, failing in such extraordinary fashion that billions of people throughout history would know his unfaithfulness. On the biggest night of human history, the guy who said he would fight to the death for Jesus was asleep when he should have been engaging in spiritual war. It is no small wonder that he folded so quickly under the pressure of the crowd.

The Christian or church that does not prioritize time with God in prayer is woefully ill-equipped for the moment. Spending time in God's presence is what prepares us to discern the spirits of the age. We are walking in some of the most deceptive and dangerous times in church history—not because someone is kicking in our doors or outlawing our beliefs but because we are being infiltrated by the seductive doctrines of man. The internal confusion and external pressures on the church are leading every believer to those moments when we are confronted like Peter was at the fire. Every believer is going to face the question: "Are you one of His?"

The Christian that does not prioritize time with God in prayer is woefully ill-equipped for the moment.

The only way we can prepare for those moments is to be people who are spiritually awake. Life is great at lulling us to sleep or filling our schedule with so many things that God is pushed aside. We become so complacent that we fail to prioritize seeking Him and appropriating the Holy Spirit's power. We may plan to start every day with prayer, but we get a cold and want to sleep in. Or we stay out late, causing us to rush through the next morning and forget our commitment. If we're not careful, we will find ourselves slumbering in the very moment when God calls us to stand.

Spiritual apathy is a killer that can be defeated only through intentionality. The thing about devotions is that they require devotion, and spiritual disciplines work only if you are disciplined enough to apply them. If we can make time in our schedules for everything else we deem important, then the only reason we wouldn't make time for God is that we must not think time with Him is all that important. Surely we know that is not the case. Be intentional in making sure you have a time and even a place set aside to meet with God. You cannot expect to sleep until the moment of the test and somehow pass it.

When we are walking in the Spirit, we become reliable in the way we respond. We are less likely to be flustered when things go wrong or to grow prideful after favorable outcomes. This levelheadedness is a direct result of relying on God and spending time with Him. It is the exact opposite of the behavior Peter exhibited.

Peter has been described as everything from hotheaded to fickle. I believe the word that best sums up his unpredictable nature is *impulsive*. Peter was impulsive. He would have done well if he'd had Paul's advice to "walk circumspectly, not as fools but as wise" (Eph. 5:15, NKJV).

Impulsiveness occurs when a person acts without thinking or by some innate compulsion. A person who walks carefully, who is acting in the spiritual fruit of self-control, cannot be guided by impulse. Impromptu and unconsidered actions occur when we are guided by the flesh. The impulsive person allows emotions to spur actions, rather than taking thoughts captive before they incite emotional response. The New Testament calls on believers to be sober and vigilant—quite the opposite of erratic, emotion-driven responses to whatever is happening in our lives. Impulsiveness can bring on poor decisions about our faith, where we worship, and even what we think we believe about God—all influenced by our emotions, as unreliable as we know them to be.

Every faith-deconstruction story tells of multiple pressures and proclivities coming together as tools Satan uses to sift us. Peter's tendencies were no different and include a bounty of lessons for every Christian. You may not have all the traits we've seen in him, but any one of them or any combination can be deadly.

THE DANGER OF WARMING AT THE WRONG FIRE

For every character flaw Peter possessed, there is a spiritual way to overcome it. But he made one mistake that's almost always deadly. As Peter began to drift from Jesus, he did not engage in conversation with other disciples. He didn't hide with some fellow Jesus follower as they both hunted a better vantage point to take in the trial. He did not flee back to the home of someone who was friendly to Christ's mission. Instead, he warmed his hands around the fires of those opposed to Jesus.

In the middle of his Rabbi's trial, Peter hung out with servants and guards of the high priest. They challenged him as one of Jesus' followers because he certainly was not one of their familiar friends. He did not belong there, and everyone knew it, but he certainly tried to fit in fast.

The Bible has many warnings about believers allowing themselves to be influenced by the wrong crowd. We are warned against relationships that involve a Christian being unequally yoked to an unbeliever. We are told that bad company corrupts good morals. These are not sayings to be quoted by Sunday school teachers and then disregarded as we grow older. The most dangerous thing believers can do is find themselves under the influence of people who are not in pursuit of Christ. If there is one piece of advice every parent, youth pastor, and student moving into new stages of life should hear, it is this: Choose your friends wisely, and choose biblically. Your friends will have a more profound influence on you than you ever imagined.

The most dangerous thing believers can do is find themselves under the influence of people who are not in pursuit of Christ.

The influence of the wrong crowd does not end with friends. In the age of the internet, our current marketplace of ideas is accessible on an unprecedented level. Through the internet terrorists have been radicalized, school shooters have been groomed, traffickers have recruited slaves, and Christians of all ages have been drawn from the faith. Yet many believers take almost no precautions in their online lives, at their own peril. In Psalm 1 we are given some very sound advice:

> Blessed is the man who walks not in the counsel
> of the ungodly, nor stands in the path of sinners,
> nor sits in the seat of the scornful; but his delight
> is in the law of the LORD, and in His law he medi-
> tates day and night. He shall be like a tree planted
> by the rivers of water, that brings forth its fruit in its
> season, whose leaf also shall not wither; and what-
> ever he does shall prosper.
>
> —PSALM 1:1–3, NKJV

Did you catch that? The psalmist is giving a description that is the exact opposite of deconstruction. Here we
do not see someone being swayed, falling apart, and collapsing under the pressure of the moment. Instead, we
see a person who grows stronger, withstands difficult
seasons, and is fruitful and righteously prosperous. This
should be the goal of every believer.

Notice that the psalmist begins with warnings about
influences. We must be careful regarding whom we hang
out with, whom we associate with on social media, and
even the websites we frequent. What begins as innocent
exploration can result in the destruction of the soul. We
can counter this by intentionally seeking out biblically
faithful Christians in our local congregations. Whom we
travel with matters.

Be careful when choosing the fires where you seek
warmth. Now would be a good time for you to examine
yourself. The next chapter can wait. Take a moment to
explore who you are. Do you have certain character flaws
that open you up to the attacks of the enemy? Has fear
or a desire to fit in stopped you from being a sold-out

Jesus follower? What about the influences in your life—which way are they pulling you? Peter did not have to deconstruct that sad night, and neither do you. If you have been slipping away from Jesus, today is a great day to start closing the distance.

Scan the QR code or visit bit.ly/4pHwzD3 to see how my daughter McKenna uses her gifts to share Jesus.

Chapter 5

REACHING THE LOW POINT

After a while someone else looked at him and said,
"You must be one of them!"
"No, man, I'm not!" Peter retorted.
—LUKE 22:58, NLT

PETER'S DECONSTRUCTION PROVIDES a fairly comprehensive look at abandoning the faith, but it lacks one element that is common to most modern deconstruction stories: We never see Peter blaming anyone else for his actions. He never declares that he stepped away from Jesus because Bartholomew treated him poorly. He never pens a letter painting Thaddeus's unloving way as the culprit in his backsliding. History doesn't record Peter delivering a flaming polemic against John, who was at the cross when Jesus died. Maybe it was because Peter had no social media accounts.

There is one place in the Scriptures where we do see Peter have a confrontation with another believer: the time Paul confronted him (Gal. 2:11). Even then, Peter's reaction was not the reaction of some of today's church people. He did not go on a tirade against Paul. He did not leave the faith or even leave ministry but remained a faithful servant of God.

It is possible he was just a product of his times, and we could dismiss the behavior of today's Christians for the same reason. Between then and now, something has changed. Individuals, and a segment of the Christian church, have begun to approach a new low; in fact, we may call it the rock bottom of deconstruction. Fewer and fewer people reject the faith because they disagree with it scientifically or struggle with its philosophical under-pinning. It is even rare for people to admit they simply have no interest in living according to biblical principles. Today, nearly everyone who rejects the faith has identified someone other than themselves who is to blame for their lack of relationship with God. They follow from a dis-tance, claiming they do so because they were forced into some noble "margin" by those who have remained close.

This has become a frequent theme in pop culture con-versations. Celebrity podcast guests may declare a deep love for the principles of Christianity and espouse the neces-sity of its teachings in the world, but before the recording is over, they inevitably proclaim they would probably be a Christian if all Christians were not so judgmental and mean. In other words, they are not following the King of kings because some Christians they know are not very nice.

These alleged almost disciples fail to mention their polyamorous relationships, their support of radical transgender ideology, or their indoctrination of their own children with thought systems antithetical to the gospel. In their view all the self-indulgence and immorality in their lives has nothing to do with their refusal to bend the knee to Christ. Nope, it is all those mean Christians. In Alabama we have a word for this: *hogwash.*

From the first time God placed moral demands on His creation, excuses have abounded for our refusal to have a relationship with Him. Rarely will you find someone who will look at you and say, "You know, God might exist, but I want to live in a way I know doesn't fit the teachings of Christianity, so I do not want to be a Christian." Instead, they will find some intellectual, philosophical, or experiential reason to explain their position—anything to avoid the real motive.

There are many in the church who parrot these favorite lines of the world. Whenever a Christian takes a bold stance on some hot-button issue, so-called Christians are often the first to chide them with warnings that this sort of action is driving people away from the church. If you speak about the moral issues of the hour, they will come up with a litany of reasons why the topic should be avoided.

Fear drove Peter to deny Christ. That same spirit of fear has driven many Christians and pastors into denying their relationship with the difficult texts and challenging points of Christianity. They are so petrified of being deemed offensive, divisive, or controversial that they no longer talk about issues the church has spoken to for centuries.

This self-censorship has created a vacuum of moral authority in the public sphere. The void is being filled by influencers, commentators, and politicians taking the place of the pulpit on matters of right and wrong. Topics that should have been ingrained in the hearts and minds of the population through teachings of the church have now been surrendered to secular authority. Family, charity, sexuality, and even the value of life itself have thus become "political" topics.

These topics were never the purview of the legislative class. Morality has always been the responsibility of the pulpit. The prophetic voice of God's kingdom speaking to the people and their leaders has provided course correction for nations throughout history—but no longer is that the case. Now when a pastor dares to speak on an issue that has been hijacked by secular authorities, other voices in his own church may rise up to silence him on the grounds that the church should avoid politics.

What they don't recognize is that their own fear of touching those subjects is leaving their people perishing for lack of understanding. Christians have become easy prey for the false teachings that are so prevalent around us because their leaders have failed to prepare them.

When they are not using the excuse of avoiding "political topics" or condemning those who do speak up as engaging in culture wars, these weak believers are seeking to convince us that offering measures of affirmation for sin is the only loving way to win the world. They contend that if all Christians were as understanding, loving, accepting, and tolerant as they are, the church would be overwhelmed by countless lost souls running to fill their pews. Ironically, their churches and organizations are almost always found to be in decline.

These self-appointed experts are the compromised Christians who always know the latest leftist lingo and progressive Christian trends. They are quick to lecture you on the proper viewpoint (theirs) on everything from addiction to homelessness to gay and transgender rights. After smugly handing you a new lexicon, they turn and refer to a confused man with augmented breasts and a five-o'clock shadow as she/her/they/them because they want to make sure they are hospitable. Their only concern for precise speech is when it is being used to virtue signal that they are the "right" kind of Christian. Any concern that our vocabulary or even what we call truth has any obligation to correspond with reality is dismissed as antiquated, restrictive, and mean.

There was a time in the church when our greatest fear was strong rebellion. While we polished our rhetoric and strengthened our apologetics against those who would wage war on our principles, we failed to recognize an invasion that was happening right under our noses. There were those in our own ranks who did not hold to the principles we were attempting to defend. The faithful church in the West is not being overthrown by the strength of our opposition. Rather, we are being undermined by the weakness of our colleagues.

Shaming and silencing truth speakers is bringing the church to a low, weak point. We wring our hands over the coarseness of those who boldly proclaim truth, while those who actively oppose basic Christian principles, espouse false doctrine, and facilitate the leftward careening of the church are celebrated for their civility. The biblical leaders who fill our sermons—men like Moses, Gideon, and Nathan—would never be allowed to stand in our pulpits. Right matters little. Niceness alone is sacred.

THE CULT OF NICENESS

This worship of *nice* has led the church into a quagmire of compromise. Recognizing that difficult topics can limit its advancement, the political class in the church world, tasked with making decisions that affect our future, will do little to confront the bad actors in our midst. Denominations are being derailed by small, vocal, unashamed groups of liberals—not because they are the majority but because those with the authority to resist have done the political math and determined that there will be peace in their day (along with honorariums, awards, travel, and prestige) as long as they "go along to get along." Throw in some great conservative-sounding rhetoric in social media posts and sermons, and the laity never even know that their beloved biblical principles are being sold out from under them.

Shaming truth speakers is bringing the church to a low, weak point.

The pirates at the helms of our commandeered

churches and institutions have learned to overlook a little bluster from leaders who try to take a conservative posture among the rank-and-file membership. Those steering the church away from truth know a little bluster means nothing. They tolerate the rhetoric in exchange for free rein when no one is looking, biding their time until full control can be realized. With a wink and nod, "conservative" leaders are deeding future generations to liberal ideologues.

The stories of tearful elderly saints lamenting the loss of their churches and denominations are heartrending. Living off the assets built by generations of faithful believers, many of today's denominations, Christian movements, Christian media, and nonprofits are becoming purveyors of a powerless gospel built on worship of self and the idolatry of niceness. Families have seen their children destroyed; congregations have seen their denominations leave them behind for more progressive worldviews. Make no mistake: Every bit of this decline in the church is made possible by the shaming and silencing of truth speakers.

Movements, when effective, are more than the sum of their parts. Yet every movement, organization, or church is a conglomeration of the individuals of which it is composed. On a large scale, we are seeing the effects of shifting blame to those who resist falsehood, forgetting that God's Word clearly places the blame for division on those who bring in false teaching. Complicity has been confused for character, and reputations are more harmed by truth-telling than sin affirmation. The cost will be the next generation of believers.

This blame shifting is simply the macro expression of what happens in the lives of individuals.

"You are the reason I don't go to church anymore."

"Christians are just mean-spirited."

"I love Jesus, but not Christians."

You may have heard all those statements. Some are probably made in sincerity, but many are not. Those who claim they cannot go to church because of Christians (but have no issue with Jesus) are probably not telling the truth—especially if they live in a place that has a variety of available congregations with whom they could worship.

Admitting you don't attend church because you don't like the accountability of being part of a fellowship is not easy. Telling others that you decided church was not for you after your last church wouldn't allow you into leadership while you lived in open sin is certainly more difficult than just saying the church had cliques. It is far easier to say you don't trust organized religion than to admit you thought your contribution should have bought you power and influence. And declaring that you love sin more than you love being in a church is certainly not an option. For many who deconstruct, the blame game becomes the norm.

Compulsive blame shifting blended with niceness-obsessed conflict avoidance has led to another viral trend in the church. Church hurt has become the go-to explanation for all manner of rebellion, backsliding, and deconstruction. This has created a world that is bad for everyone—those who have left the church and those who have remained. Obsessing over church hurt has become an excuse for the unrepentant and a muzzle for those tasked with speaking truth.

There's no denying that church hurt does happen. Wherever there are people, someone is going to do something wrong, mistakes are going to be made, and feelings are going to be hurt. Family hurt happens. Workplace hurt happens. Sports-team hurt happens. Human contact means conflict is going to occur, and the result is often hurt. But this reality is no validation for abandoning the faith or forsaking the church.

People never swear off work because they got their feelings hurt by a manager ten years ago. No therapist ever looks at a patient and says, "You should abandon the idea of family for the rest of your life because a family member hurt you." We do not refuse to enter any restaurant again because one restaurant's server was rude. Yet we are expected to believe that untold numbers of people are essentially unreachable by the gospel because they were hurt by one Christian or one group of Christians out of the billions of Christians and hundreds of thousands of congregations in the world. *Gaslighting* is an overused term in our world, but it sure seems to fit here.

I understand that people get hurt in church. Still, we must be very careful what we label as church hurt. Accountability is not church hurt. Leadership standards are not church hurt. Biblical pastoral instruction is not church hurt. Rebuke of sin is not church hurt. Reproof is not church hurt. These are flesh hurts. These truths hurt our flesh. That is a good thing. One of the purposes of gathering is that we can get help in crucifying our flesh. As one pastoral saying goes, "We're here to comfort the afflicted and afflict the comfortable."

In today's church Paul would be scolded, be derided by cowardly colleagues, and probably become the subject of a very unflattering Netflix documentary.

Paul assured Timothy that all Scripture is God-breathed and "profitable for doctrine, for reproof, for correction, for instruction in righteousness" (2 Tim. 3:16, NKJV). In this verse the apostle provided a list of the proper uses of the Scriptures in the church. Sadly, that very list would create all manner of hurt in our modern churches. Doctrine is too divisive. Reproof is mean and hypocritical. Correction is judgmental. Instruction in righteousness is pharisaical and religious. What is the modern pastor left with? Smile, affirm, and bless whatever sin or confusion your people are living in. Give them a good dose of sweet spiritual morphine to dull the conscience and ease the mind. Oh, and hope they don't recognize you in hell.

If Pauline instructions to a young pastor are not usable in our congregations, then we have a real problem. Of course, Paul would never be accepted in the modern, dying, compromised church. He talked about people being under God's curse; kicked a man out of the church for sexual immorality; said the lazy should not eat; called a whole culture lying, brutish, lazy gluttons; and even spoke in crude terms of the Judaizers who perverted the gospel. In today's church Paul would be scolded, be derided by cowardly colleagues, and probably become the subject of a very unflattering Netflix documentary.

It is no small wonder that deconstructionists and progressive Christians have little regard for Paul; many of them dismiss his writing completely. Intellectual honesty would require that they apply the same standard to Jesus. As paradoxical as it may sound, there is no way our weak, apostate churches would accept the things He taught during His ministry.

Jesus called religious leaders vipers and white-washed tombs, chastised Peter as "Satan," and told whole cities they were doomed for hell. He used illustrations that involved throwing people out of gatherings because they did not wear the right garment, servants being beaten, and a risk-averse steward being called wicked and lazy. He once compared a pleading woman with a dog and cursed a fig tree for not bearing fruit. He responded to a son wanting to attend his father's funeral with, "Let the dead bury their own dead" (Matt. 8:22). He even called for the violent killing of those who cause harm to little ones. If today's progressive church has a problem with Paul, they most certainly find Jesus, at least as He is described in the Gospels, repulsive. Perhaps that's why they are so keen to elevate experiential revelation over biblical exegesis. Jesus can be whatever you want Him to be when you create Him in your own mind.

STOP REWRITING JESUS

This is the crux of the issue. For the vast majority of people who apostatize, their reasons have more to do with their own desires and moral decisions than with the church or other people. Some simply cannot give up their autonomy. Others have issues with Christianity because someone they care about is involved in sin. Ultimately, the real issue is the moral demands that come with believing in God and embracing Christ as Lord.

Who then can they blame? It cannot be Jesus. That is a bridge too far. So they make Jesus into a really nice guy who makes no demands other than "judge not." Once Jesus has been transformed into this false Christ, all genuine Christians become jerks. "I'm not the problem. Jesus is not the problem. Church is the problem."

This excuse could work—if not examined. And many are getting away with it. However, there's an obvious problem. The only way one can arrive at this position is to misrepresent Jesus.

One summer day, some friends and I were out swimming at a lake that was a favorite summer hangout. Swimming was one of the best ways to relieve those hot South Florida days when the air felt like a wet blanket and even the alligators were looking for shade. We also enjoyed diving down and looking at the cars, stolen from Miami, that had found their way to the lake bottom. That day, as we hung out, talked, dove, and enjoyed a great time, the conversation took a turn that would impact me for the rest of my life.

"You know, Jesus is a Son of God, but not *the* God."

My friend knew I was a pastor's son, and somehow our meandering conversation had wound from cars, sports, and girls to religion. I knew that he was a Jehovah's Witness and that our families had different beliefs, but we had never really gotten into them. That statement that Jesus was not God caught my full attention. He went on to point out that his "Bible" phrased John 1:1 differently from the wording in my Bible. Based on this, he informed me, my view of Jesus was wrong.

This was a pretty substantive claim. If he was right about Jesus, that meant my dad was wrong, my granddad was wrong, and so many Christians I knew and went to church with were all wrong about Jesus. At that moment, I could have just dismissed him and continued believing what I had been taught. I could have taken his instruction and converted to his faith. However, neither of those was an option for me. I had to research it for myself. I was too skeptical to accept anything at face value.

I purchased an interlinear Bible; I wanted to see the words in their original language. I started researching his claims, comparing the text of his Bible translation against the Greek and Hebrew in the interlinear. I also started digging into his beliefs and the people behind them.

The Jehovah's Witness doctrine is so flimsy that it did not take long to see through it. Not only was their own Bible inconsistent in the way it handled texts about Jesus, but I discovered that Charles Taze Russell, the founder of the cult, had been proved a fraud in open court when, despite his claims of biblical linguistic expertise, he was unable to recognize Greek and Hebrew texts. After spending time investigating my friend's assertions, I was able to dismiss them as unsubstantiated and came out with my Christian faith stronger than ever.

I have carried that same willingness to investigate truth claims throughout my entire life. When I am faced with a new ideology or worldview, I weigh it against what I know and examine its credibility. Then I know whether it is something to be embraced or rejected. I look for truth and stand where I find it because truth is all that's dependable in our ever-shifting world. I am never easily convinced, but when I get there, I am super convinced.

When it comes to Jesus, there can be no in-between. Claims concerning Him are absolute and are among the easiest ways to discern the veracity of any thought system. Every false belief structure mishandles Jesus, from various perversions of Christianity to other world religions to political science. If they get Jesus wrong, do not trust them on anything else.

As already discussed, progressive Christianity has terribly mishandled Jesus. They have completely overlooked anything hard that He said and will even claim He never addressed issues like sexuality and other moral topics. Yet biblical history shows that Jesus directly affirmed the Genesis creation order and rejected modern transgender ideology. He discussed sexuality, monogamy, and divorce. Jesus defended private property rights and rejected the seizure of others' property as forced charity. Again and again, He took positions that absolutely reject progressive Christianity's attempts to make Him an LGBTQ-affirming, polyamory-supporting Marxist. Despite the evidence, take your seat among the dwindling crowd at one of the compromised churches, and you will likely hear them claiming Jesus is the woke hero He never was.

To assist in making Jesus in their own image, some Christians have developed an unhealthy interest in red-letter teaching, or red-letter Christianity. While I understand using His words as a basis for a sermon series or study, we should be aware of a danger that lurks in dismissing or subordinating the rest of Scripture. All Scripture is the God-breathed, infallible Word of God. There is not one command, punishment, warning, or incident of God's wrath with which Christ disagrees. Remember, the whole Bible is God speaking, not just subsets of direct quotes.

Progressive Christians do the same thing cults have done throughout the ages: They mishandle Jesus. Muslims do the same thing, making Him a subordinate prophet. The dangerous difference is that you probably will not sit under the preaching of a rabbi, cult leader, or imam, but chances are you will encounter some progressive Christians in the pulpit or leading a group. This is when being spiritually awake becomes so vital to our survival.

While they are not as far from truth as their liberal

counterparts, we should also be aware of Christless conservatism, particularly in Western nations. As people have grown weary of the radical leftist agendas being forced on us, many are turning to conservatism and its commonsense defense of societal norms. Christians should be aware that among the voices you may agree with on personal liberty and certain social issues, there are also many dangerous and antichrist views. When you begin to hear antisemitism, personal autonomy even in antisocial behaviors, conservative homosexuality, pro-abortion argumentation, and even Christ as merely an archetype or point of philosophical interest, be very careful. Christ is either personal Savior and Lord in all areas, including obedience to the moral demands of Scripture, or He is being mishandled.

Misrepresenting Jesus to separate Him from the church and put distance between Him and His moral teaching is all a carefully crafted strategy of Satan. The old serpent is fine with people having a relationship with Jesus, just not the real Jesus. He knows that since Eden, humankind has been given to shifting blame. If we can blame others, the church, and truth seekers, or if we can re-create Jesus into our own image, then our deconstruction is not our fault. Blame the church. Blame Jesus. Just do not blame the person who denies the faith.

It's not hard to see how absurd it is to blame others for our decisions regarding Christianity. If you want to live by your own moral standard, just say so. If you do not like accountability, then be honest about it. There is less shame in openly declaring you want to live life your own way than to continue blaming others for your decisions. Only when you're honest about how you arrived at your current conclusions can you really evaluate whether they are the right ones.

You may not be the person who has left the faith, but there may be someone you know or love who is deconstructing. You have my heartfelt empathy. I know the pain of seeing people I care deeply for fall into deception, and I know how difficult it is when they begin to see you as the enemy. Be encouraged: There is a path forward.

First, you must maintain your own integrity. Maintain your unity with Christ, and do not come into agreement with their sin. God's Word offers blessings for those who are in unity with Him and stark warnings for agreeing with sin. While you may have relational ties to an apostate person, you must be careful not to come across as affirming their sin, validating them as a Christian while they pursue immorality, or wavering in your commitment to God's truth. It is quite possible to love a wandering friend without throwing out your convictions.

Countless times, I have seen parents and grandparents cosign the destructive decisions of their children. Whether it be celebrating a gay wedding or providing for cohabitation, somehow they think that embracing their loved one's sin is an act of love. Supporting someone you care about in their sin is like clapping for them as they drunkenly pull out of your driveway and head the wrong direction on the interstate. It is never loving to celebrate decisions that will destroy their lives and others'.

It is also important for you to make a clear decision. You must decide whether you actually think the sin in question is destructive. Do you truly believe it will ruin lives and send people to hell? Do you think it incurs God's wrath? Do you really believe people need to repent and turn from their sins to follow after Christ? In other words, you must determine whether you really believe what you have always claimed to believe.

Rewriting the Scripture is not an option. Making Jesus into some other religious figure who supports your whims and desires—or those of your loved one—is not on the table. You have to decide. Do you believe what the Bible says, or do you not?

If you say, "Yes, I believe God's Word," then accepting sin is not an option for you. It is certainly not loving. In fact, it is among the most hateful things you could ever do; it pushes people toward hell. Remember, the moment you leave the truth, you lose your ability to help bring people back to it. So be wise with your boundaries and grace-filled in your connections.

There is also the possibility that a person reading this book could be dealing with deconstruction in their own heart. If that is you, if you have begun to question the teachings of Scripture or think God's demands are out-dated, you're not alone. Many other believers have dealt with the same questions and found themselves stronger in faith after overcoming their doubts. Find a brother or sister in Christ, and begin to open up about your questions and concerns. They may not have the answers, which is OK. You can seek out a faithful teacher or pastor and find the answers together. Trust me, you are not asking a question that some great Christian has not already found a way to answer. Satan has been telling the same lies for centuries—but the truth always prevails.

Be open to the soft truth about yourself. Are you blaming others for your drift, when it is really about your own desires? Are you struggling with some things about yourself? That too is OK. God has enough grace for every struggle, and the gospel is powerful to transform every life. Be open to the Holy Spirit. Seek God. Find the places where you may be drifting, and begin to close the distance with Jesus. The bad news is, no one else can be blamed for your walk with God. The good news is, no one else is responsible for your walk with God. It's between you and the Lord.

He waits with open arms.

Scan the QR code or visit bit.ly/ 487IL9I to join the (Un)Embarrassed of Jesus Facebook group.

Chapter 6

THE PRODIGAL CHURCH IS COMING TO ITS SENSES

So he returned home to his father. And while he was still a long way off, his father saw him coming. Filled with love and compassion, he ran to his son, embraced him, and kissed him.
—LUKE 15:20, NLT

IT STANK. IT seemed a lifetime had passed since he stopped noticing the smell.

The sounds were always there, the rooting, grunting, chewing, flatulence, and occasional angry squeal. The slimy muck was there too, made by the buckets of water he carried from the well and poured into a corner of the lot, ensuring there was always a place for the pigs to cover themselves with mud. The sights never really changed. A few pigs in and a few out, but everything else stayed the same. The smell, though, was gone—until today.

After the morning feeding, he had wandered a little

farther and longer from the pigpen than he normally did. His thoughts that day had been all over the place. Life had not been great lately, but that could change. Maybe, if he could work a few months and scrape up a few coins, his lot would change. His dad was a successful businessman, and if that old fogy could do it—with all his antiquated ways, outdated methods, and even giving away 10 percent of his profits to the temple—he knew he could do better. His brother may have been the favorite, but he would show them all.

Those thoughts were a pleasant fantasy but little more. His pay was not even enough to cover the cost of a place to live, so he had taken to sleeping alongside the pigs. On those cool desert nights, when the sun dropped behind the mountains and the dry air gave up all its heat, he was even thankful for them. His mind, trained in accounting by his father's bookkeeper, rolled through the calculations. A few more months, and maybe he could make it out of here. He just needed to save.

What was he going to save? He hadn't had a new set of clothes in nearly a year. The only pair of sandals he owned needed repair; his good ones had been stolen off his feet as he lay sleeping after a raucous night of cheap wine and debauchery. That was all right—he could wait a little longer for a robe and some shoes.

His stomach grumbled at him, but he had no answer for its complaints. There was no chance of a warm meal until he got paid, but that was the day after tomorrow. He would see if there were some scraps in the pig slop that did not look too bad. Last week, he had found a treasure.

Some careless kitchen servants had thrown away nearly a dozen figs that were barely beginning to rot. Yesterday, there had been half an onion with just a touch of mold on it. Who knew what today might bring?

Then it happened. The smell was there. That day, the pigpen stunk again, and the tiniest look of disgust crossed his face. It was not because he was above being around the smell of animals; he had helped around his father's farm since he was a boy. His earliest memories were of tagging along as his dad checked on his property and visited with his servants. He could remember the first time he'd been left with the staff to work throughout the day. His father could not abide the thought of raising a son with no work ethic, and he wanted his boys to be familiar with the workings of the estate that would one day be theirs.

He could remember his mother demanding that he wash up after those days afield. There was no way she was going to let one of her boys sit down to dinner reeking like that. She kept a nice home, full of the smells of herbs, spices, and various incense, a stark difference from the stench of the sheepfold and cow pens. Something in him missed that—not just the scents of good food and a clean home but the contrast of those smells against the others.

On the day he had come to inquire about working here, the stink had been one of the first things he noticed. He had never been around pigs; none of his family or their friends would have ever raised such filthy, unlawful creatures. The smell and the defiance of Jehovah would have been putrid to his sensibilities if he had had any left. The last of his dignity had been drowned by the vinegar (they said it was wine) some kind soul had given him a few days after the last of his money had run dry.

Something happened when he got this job. After a few hours he stopped noticing the stench. Then when he left and returned, it was there again, a reminder of just how far he had fallen. Over time it stopped coming and going. Maybe it was because it was so ingrained in his clothes and skin that he never really left it behind. Whatever the reason, it did not stink anymore.

Until today.

As he topped the last hill, he was met by a welcome breeze. The stirring air would make his outdoor life—unless you counted the lean-to pig shelter as indoors—a little more tolerable. As the air stirred, for the first time in as long as he could remember, the pigpen stank again. With the breeze and the smell, something else swept over the wayward young man. He found himself longing for the home he had left behind, the structure he had so despised, and the father he had scorned. When that smell hit his nostrils, he remembered. He did not belong here.

~

Jesus' story of the prodigal son (Luke 15:11–32) is one of the most discussed illustrative parables in all Scripture. Tens of thousands of sermons have been built on this tale of youthful mistakes, needless misfortune, enduring love, and incredible grace. You have probably heard a few of them yourself. You may have even told the story to someone who had fallen into sin and was ashamed of returning to God for forgiveness. What a story it is!

We call him the prodigal because of his reckless, wasteful spending. His story resonates with most of us because we have all been guilty of not recognizing how good the love of the Father is. We know what it is to have taken His blessings for granted, wasting time and resources on self-serving endeavors that leave us empty and regretful. All of us have been blessed by having a heavenly Father whose love for us has never been swayed by the foolishness of our decisions.

As we look at the story of the wayward son, we see parallels to the modern church. There are many strong, truth-preaching churches that are experiencing growth and revival; there is also a disturbing number that have followed the path of the prodigal. Entire denominations have departed from the tried-and-true paths and wandered far from home, becoming unrecognizable shells of their storied histories.

Those leading the prodigal church have demanded the reins of historically conservative biblical churches. A generation arose that has little regard for the people who labored so diligently to build the platforms on which they now stand. For them any semblance of the past is antiquated and to be dismissed. They look down on biblical inerrancy, dismiss orthodox views of sin and salvation, and even scoff at the need for evangelizing the lost. Rather than being a place where believers can hear the gospel, be strengthened by Christian fellowship, and be discipled by sound teaching, the prodigal church focuses on acceptance and affirmation, prioritizing social justice and promoting secular progressive theories. Deceived by the call of the far country—the appeal of being palatable to the world—they've stepped out of the Father's gate of truth and descended the path of relativism toward destruction.

The prodigalizing of church has led to incredible loss in physical terms as well. While we know the kingdom of God is not measured in buildings, acres, or bank accounts, these metrics are another measure of the progressive Christian movement's gutting of the church.

Church that does not challenge believers is as pointless as a gym where no exercise is allowed.

Take a moment and check out what has happened to the "seeker-sensitive" church. This Sunday, click on the live stream of the gay-affirming mainline church in your town. They probably own one of the most beautiful buildings in the city, sitting at one of the most desirable locations. Yet their pews are empty.

Church that does not challenge believers is as pointless as a gym where no exercise is allowed. What is the point of membership? When you remove the transformative power of the gospel, Christianity loses its appeal. When our faith becomes centered on improving the temporal well-being of society, we become, as Paul said, people who have hope only in this life and are miserable as a result. Organizations that once fed the spirit and changed the eternal trajectory of the soul have largely abandoned that work, and people can tell the difference.

The progressive church finds itself in a terrible predicament. After years of aligning with God-hating ideologies and self-serving worldviews, these churches are slowly dying. They seem shocked that people whose movements are built on personal autonomy, sexual perversion, and utopian fantasies would not see a church's pro-LGBT flag or pro-transgender sermon and come running in to bend the knee to Christ. The accumulated resources of generations have been squandered in an attempt to align with anti-God forces—and very few souls have been won.

The traditional, long-standing members of these churches are left with little choice. They love their churches, including the property, buildings, and fixtures they poured so much into developing. They also see that their beloved churches have left them. Many feel alienated. As they share their concerns, the churches experience schism and, ultimately, exodus. Cities across the Western world are now awash in beautiful, empty buildings where mere handfuls still gather—unless they have not already sold the properties to bars, clubs, or restaurants.

The prodigal, progressive church is responsible for the theft of millions of dollars from hardworking saints. Even more serious, it is responsible for the destruction of millions of souls who have been deceived and many more who have not heard the gospel because of their pastors' dereliction. For many of these churches, it seems there is no positive change coming. For those misled souls, however, there is good news.

The prodigal church does not describe the entire

church. Yes, there are many who have abandoned truth. There are cowards who fill pulpits and lead men and women to destruction because they are afraid to challenge them with a call to repentance. There are certainly denominations, institutions, and movements that have become apostate. But there are also some who are faithful.

A STIRRING IN THE MUD

Something is happening in the church. There is a stirring of the Holy Spirit in the hearts of men and women. While some have been muzzled by fear, there is also a growing number of bold truth speakers who are not embarrassed by their faith. While you may see online videos of Christians explaining away the hard texts of the Bible, there is probably a biblically sound church within driving distance of your home. Chances are it is one of the only churches growing in your town. They have smelled the stench of where the church has gone and are refusing to let it remain wallowing in the mud.

Something is happening in the church. There is a growing number of bold truth speakers who are not embarrassed by their faith.

As I travel the country speaking, engaging, and meeting with leaders, my heart has become encouraged. I am meeting more and more church leaders and laity who, like the prodigal, have looked around and realized that the church has been led somewhere it does not belong. We are the truth people, the life-changing gospel people, the Jesus-will-set-you-free people. These Christians recognize that, and they are changing their world.

When the prodigal son realized how far he had fallen, he immediately began to take steps toward the father's house. He knew that the place he was in did not match the way he had been raised. He recognized just how wasteful he had been, and he could not get home fast enough.

We see that same thing happening in the church. Years of polite, Christian-lite, diet religion has sapped the energy from the church. It has emptied pews, stolen the power from preaching, and left altars barren. Furthermore, it has decimated institutions in our society.

Without a grounded belief in God, Western society does not work. You cannot expect those who do not know God to steward properly the freedoms we've enjoyed. Without God's natural created order, civilization cannot last. Thus, we have seen the erosion of family, morality, and society happening at a record pace. This is made possible only because of the anemic pulpits that have too long steered our church.

When a society decides that a mother and father raising their children together in a stable, traditional home is no longer necessary, they are deluded. Statistics are clear: This is the absolute best setting in which a child can be raised. The only reason we would reject that truth is because of the moral implications that come along with it. In a world where everything is relative, we can no longer even say that one situation is better than another. That is foolish and destructive. If I am in the middle of a hurricane on the ocean, I am sure an aircraft carrier is a better vessel than a pool float. Yet if someone speaks of what is best for children, they are called judgmental and antiquated. If the pulpit had done its job, this would not be the case.

When we normalize behaviors outside God's norm, we undermine the very fabric of society. When a grown man wants to dress like a seminude woman and dance in front of children, that is not normal. If a child decides they are an animal, a sane society does not buy them a tail and a collar; we get them to a counselor. When a man wants to box a woman, we tell him to fight the men or go home. No functioning society can spend its resources to promote and pursue the delusions of every perversion that comes along without disrupting the pillars on which we stand. Again, much of the fault for our decay lies in the pulpit. It is up to the church to declare truth, not to wait for secular researchers or social commentators to approve our position. Let God's Word be true, and every man a liar.

But something good is happening in the world. People are beginning to awaken to the reality that we've been living in absurdity, and they are looking for a place to get answers. The only place with viable answers is the Christ-honoring, Bible-teaching church. Even the *New York Post* has acknowledged a notable influx of young people coming into the church.[1] In a world where reality seems like shifting sand, where every article may be written by AI and every video could be a deepfake, people are crying out for something real, something solid. The church and God's Word have what they need, if we are bold enough to give it to them.

One of the biggest shifts in the church is happening

among men. For some time the church has been led by women. I'm not talking about who has the title of pastor or who can be appointed to organizational leadership; I am referring to the actual happenings at the local church. It has been women who prayed, women who were most involved in worship, and women who carried the fire of the Holy Spirit. While most congregations may have had a few men with hearts for God, many were going through the motions, if that much.

For too long the church has been a church without men, and when they were there, many of them were so emasculated that the average man would run from such a faith. Men need a challenge—they need something bold, they need something to conquer—and Christianity was telling them to be polite, to affirm what they knew was not true, and to be nice at all costs, no matter how bad things got. Men did not want this. It did not resonate with them. It failed to connect with their God-given design and left their spirits unstirred. So they left the church in droves.

This is changing.[2] Men have begun to recognize that the world around them is falling apart. They see their children walking in confusion and recognize it's their job to do something about it. Some have turned to secular voices for guidance in everything from raising children to making sense of the times, but these voices can only do so much. These men need something more. They need God—and they are starting to find Him.

The feminist movement took the Western world by storm. Someone convinced women that they had been held back far too long by the norms of society. The patriarchy had been unbearable. Who were these men who wanted to provide for and protect them while they bore children, kept homes, and engaged in the oppressive activities of family life? How dare men hold women back? Did they not realize that every woman's dream was to work on an assembly line with a bunch of stinking, cussing, vulgar men? Or to cater to every whim of her executive boss while her own husband would have to make do without her?

The feminist movement has backfired. Sure, a woman can make money. She can be the boss. She can be independent and let every man know she is her own woman. She can even be promiscuous. Why not?

She is finding out. Marriage rates are down. Birth rates are down. This is incredibly sad for the women in our society. Studies have revealed that the absolute happiest and most fulfilled women are those who are married and raising children.[3] No other category comes close. The bad news for the feminist movement is that, while they gained what they thought they wanted, they have lost what really made them happy. Many women with successful careers, résumés full of accomplishments, and empty homes have learned that men were just looking for wives and partners. The value of a virtuous woman is at an all-time high.

RESTORATION OF GOD'S BEAUTIFUL DESIGN

Thankfully, young Christians are beginning to see the beauty of marriage again. There is a generation rising that recognizes God's way is best, for them and for the society they are part of. Young men are being drawn to this, recognizing that part of their role is to be a responsible citizen and part of a church. Christ-honoring young men are hearing the call to be loving husbands and fathers, living lives that glorify God through the most basic of His commands and following His design.

These young men are stepping into their roles as leaders in the church and community. For the first time in recent memory, surveys reveal that young men are more religious than young women. They are buying more Bibles, attend church more regularly, and are more likely to identify as religious.[4] These young men aren't returning to churches that shrink back from the truth. Instead, they are seeking out bold churches with brave leaders who will stand and declare the truth—God's truth. A stark contrast to the dying, compromised, progressive church, these congregations are vibrant, growing, and full of revival.

The prodigal son recognized his mistake. Some in the prodigal church have done the same. Some well-meaning pastors got caught up in the seeker-sensitive, offend-no-one, motivational-speech, concert-and-sermonette style of church. The Holy Spirit has begun to convict these leaders. They are turning back to God-honoring, Bible-teaching ministry where the gospel is preached, sin is confronted, and discipleship is at the center of everything. And it is working.

It does not make sense to pursue God with anything less than a whole heart. Intuitively, we all understand this. A faith that demands nothing, that changes nothing, that has no impact on believers and unbelievers, is worthless. Christians know this. Those who have been born again are hungry for discipleship. They are inspired by boldness. We should be giving them healthy doses of both.

As teachers were inside preparing for the school year at Mary G. Montgomery High School in Mobile, something else was happening on the outside. Students began to show up: some driving, others dropped off by parents. At first there were a few, then ten, then more. Soon they had a large, diverse gathering from every social group in the school. It is a strange thing to get students to show up a week before school starts, but here they were. They did not assemble for a program or a sports event. Instead, they gathered to walk. They walked once around the property, prayed, then got in their vehicles or called their rides, and returned home.

This happened for the next six days. On the seventh day, the first day of school, they did something different. They walked around the school property *seven times*. Then they prayed again. By this day, there were dozens of them, gathering before daylight, before the rooster crowed, not to deny but to boldly declare that they were *unembarrassed of Jesus* and that in this school the kingdom of God would be present.

The students called it the "Jericho Walk." Out of this group of kids came so many incredible stories, I could fill a whole book with them. We call them our Jesus Revolution Kids. If you come to Pathway Church, you'll find them sitting on the front rows, and not because someone told them to be there. They'll have their Bibles open, taking notes and making highlights, soaking up the gospel and how to walk closely with the Lord.

During worship they fill the altar in prayer. Everywhere they go, they go boldly, declaring Jesus to anyone who will listen and to some who will probably try not to.

This movement really started with a kid named Dallas, whom you met in an earlier chapter. He attended church at one of our campuses, and someone invited him to youth camp. When he asked a staff member if he could go, he was informed that the camp was full. But he persisted. Finally, someone told him he could go but would have to sleep on the floor. He agreed. That week, Dallas had a radical salvation experience. He now serves on our staff at Pathway.

The so-called experts would tell you this should not have happened. At the time, I sat with my staff and explained that God was calling us to be bold on the difficult issues of the day. I let them know I wanted every staff member, teacher, and department to be bold and unashamed of the gospel, including the difficult topics. This never drove anyone away; it drew young people to us. It was unlike anything they were getting anywhere else. Finally, someone was giving them truth.

It was in that environment that Dallas began his journey as a believer. He was a radical from the beginning, and his zeal was contagious. Dallas was an athlete with a winsome personality. When he showed up to youth worship and went straight to the front to worship and pray, others started joining him. On Sunday when he walked in with his Bible and started sitting on the front row, it was not long before several rows were filled with other hungry young believers. A bold youth program resulted in a bold convert, which has led to bold action, which has grown the kingdom.

That is how it works when we refuse to be ashamed of Jesus!

One day, Dallas walked into my office and sat down. I had seen God's work in his life and was curious to hear what he had to say. With no appointment or call, he informed me that he wanted to hold a student worship and testimony night at the high school. I looked at this kid whom I could not help but love and believe in and told him to go for it. With Dallas, I knew he would make it work.

He spoke with someone about permission to hold the event, and then he and his friends started promoting the night. Gen Z is a different breed. Their marketing was straightforward and looked almost clunky next to the slick designs we'd grown accustomed to. When I saw their poster, which they had designed using *Time* magazine's Jesus Revolution cover as their inspiration, I hoped their night would live up to that incredible movement decades ago. The marketer in me was more than a little concerned with their choice of name. It was terrible: "Student Worship and Testimony Night." Who was going to come to that?

Apparently, everyone.

On the night of the event, the auditorium was full—more than seven hundred students. It was everything Dallas and his group of co-organizers (each now as radical as he) had hoped for. With no adult involvement, students led worship, shared testimonies, and conducted every part of the service, including a sermon by Dallas.

That night more than one hundred students gave their lives to Christ, and at least seventy were baptized—because a handful of bold teens were too bold to fail.

One day, as Dallas and I were chatting, he mentioned the Jericho Walk. When we talked about the seventh day, I said, "And the walls fell down!"

"Not physical walls, Pastor Travis, but the spiritual ones sure did. A lot of people got saved that year."

One bold church. One bold convert. One bold youth group. One bold action. One school turned upside down for Jesus.

The prodigal church is returning home. We've seen what has been wasted. We know that where we've been is not where our heavenly Father meant us to be. Fear, polite Christianity, progressive ideology, and every other rotten thing are being left back at the pigpen.

No longer following from a distance.

No longer afraid.

No longer silent.

Go get the robe, the ring, and the new shoes.

The *unembarrassed* church is coming home.

Scan the QR code or visit bit.ly/4o0VDmV to learn how to take bold faith and care to one child who needs your help.

PART III

FOLLOWING JESUS, CHANGING THE WORLD

Chapter 7

HOPE FOR THE CHURCH

*But his father said to the servants, "Quick! Bring
the finest robe in the house and put it on him. Get
a ring for his finger and sandals for his feet."*
—LUKE **15:22**, NLT

IT IS INCREASINGLY evident that the Christian church is
coming to its senses.

Decades of decline in religious affiliation have halted
as faithful congregations fill up with hungry believers.
Young people yearning for meaning are expressing
interest in discipleship that surpasses that of past generations. A major shift in Western Christianity is occurring
as mainline apostate churches are being emptied by a generation that longs for transcendent, unchanging truth.

Pastors are having different conversations. While
some are still caught up in the consumer-based model of
church growth, a growing number have seen through the
facade. Their focus has shifted from trying to appeal to

larger numbers of people to growing individual believers in their walk with Christ. Pulpits are ringing with the truth that there is no king but King Jesus and that following Him requires total commitment.

Churches that have rounded off the edges of the gospel are in decline. People today care less about marketing and more about whether a fellowship is going to help them navigate the difficult topics they deal with in their families, homes, and businesses. Fathers are refusing to bring their families to sit under an effeminate self-help specialist who trips over himself to avoid saying anything that might ruffle feathers. Mothers are recognizing that Satan is out to destroy their children and that the only hope is for them to be called from their sin, not comforted in it. They want something that the dying, compromised church cannot offer.

A positive result of the world's lurch toward absurdity is that it revealed the extent to which ludicrous and evil ideologies have infiltrated the world. When parents can lose custody over refusing to accommodate their child's sterilization, people begin to wake up. When laws are passed that a school can facilitate a gender change or encourage a child to pursue homosexuality, without informing the parents, people begin to wake up. When girls' trophies are handed to mediocre male athletes, people can see that something is wrong.

We have gone beyond the pale regarding natural order and basic institutions of society, and it has come with a cost. Depression, suicide, and despair have risen to record numbers among people who were once the hope of the future. As ideologies have spiraled further into irrationality, things have grown more dismal. Reacting to this, we are beginning to see the proverbial pendulum swing away from some of the radical positions that have been too long unchecked.

Secular society has begun to arrive at positions God's church has long held. Marriage is good. Children do best with two biological parents raising them in a loving home. Charity happens most efficiently, with the least fraud and waste, when conducted freely and not compelled by the government. Nations should have borders. Radical sexual reorientation and gender-bending ideology are devastating to the mental health of young people. Abortion is destructive to life in the womb and to the adults involved. Nations do better when biblical principles are included in the education of their children. People are responsible for their own actions and must be held accountable. To Christians these are not novel ideas; they are Bible. They are truth.

We have the answer for every situation around us. You can investigate every failing aspect of a nation, state, city, family, or individual, and they will all have one thing in common: failure to live by our loving Creator's design for people and society. When God and His Word are embraced and lived out, we can correct or prevent those problems. Just as the Holy Spirit moved across the void of the earth and set things in order, when He begins to work in us, things begin to be set in order.

Churches that recognize this reality are poised to see continued growth. Christianity works. Individual believers and their families who turn to the basic tenets of historic Christianity will find that their lives immediately begin to change for the better. This is not self-help; it's dependence on God's Word and the Holy Spirit's guidance. It's not a superstitious gospel; it's the simple principle that God knows best and wants what's best for us.

Kingdom leaders who recognize the gap between where the church has been and where God calls us to be can find encouragement in Christ's story of the returning prodigal. When the wayward son came home, he was prepared to settle for being treated as a servant in his father's fields. He believed he had relinquished his right to be called a son, that his mistakes had irreparably cost him the authority and blessing of his birthright. In many relationships that would be the case. Thankfully, our heavenly Father is loving and forgiving.

Jesus painted a beautiful picture of the returning prodigal. The young man began his journey home with no thought of restoration, but when the father saw him, everything changed. While he was still "a long way off," the father noticed him and had compassion (Luke 15:20). He recognized his son and had no thought of rejection or resentment—only mercy and joy.

Those who have found themselves far from God's truth can be thankful for this moment. Maybe someone you love became involved in sin, and rather than standing for truth, you affirmed their decisions. It could be that your heart to help others let you accept Marxist-like ideas that run counter to biblical truth. Anything, from your personal feelings to the appeal of a friend to the constant influx of lying media, could have led you to accept things that, deep in your spirit, you knew were not true. The good news is you've recognized that where you are is not where God meant you to be. The better news is that you do not have to stay there. You can return to the Father, repent, and ask the Holy Spirit to guide you in truth and righteousness. You can come home.

The prodigal had not even made it all the way home when his father came running to him. Those who have been influenced by the spirit of the age may have a very long road back to orthodoxy. When you've allowed your thinking to be guided by so many voices that are antithetical to Scripture, it can be difficult to untangle from all that. Thankfully, the Father will meet you where you are.

Remember, as I learned from Blake's trip in my truck, it matters whom you travel with. If you find yourself following the wrong leader and heading for the wrong place, do something about it. This may sound radical, but it is far better to lose a relationship than to lose your soul. If you recognize that you have friends or spiritual leaders who are leading you away from biblical Christianity, do something about it. It's possible to confront them about where they're wrong and rejoice with them as they return from falsehood. If they will not return, then walk away. If hanging out with them, being in their small group, or attending their church is putting your faith at risk or confusing your values and your family, then find someone else to be your travel companion. It matters too much to do any less.

It is crucial to identify the things in your own thinking

that are contrary to God's ways. This happens only through spending time with God and with good influences. Find a faithful group of believers who are unafraid to stand for truth. Run with them. Look around for the role models God is putting in your life. The Father will come to meet the prodigal, and He often does it by placing the right influences in their proximity.

THE FIRST STEP BACK TO GOD

When the father encountered the prodigal, he embraced him. I believe this father and son walked arm in arm back to the father's house. The first step to returning from a journey we've taken into the far country is to reestablish and rebuild closeness with God. The only way to be who He designed us to be is to put intimacy with God above everything else.

It is crucial to identify the things in your own thinking that are contrary to God's ways.

When you think about what drove the prodigal son into rebellion, there are many possibilities. It could be that he didn't get along with his brother. Maybe he fell in among some bad influences. Whatever the reason, the only way he became a prodigal was to allow distance between himself and his father.

Had the young man spent more time with his dad, walking, talking, and learning all he could, the story could have been much different. Maybe some decisions were made that he did not agree with, but if he had known his father's reasoning, he could have understood why things were handled the way they were. If he didn't want to wait for his inheritance but had known his father's heart, he would have trusted his father's timing. If that relationship had been stronger, it's likely he never would have felt the need to head to the far country.

There is one surefire way to avoid becoming a prodigal, and it is going to sound familiar. Stay close to the Father. If you are a returning prodigal, do everything you can to get as close as possible to Him as fast as you can. Spend time reading and learning the Word, dedicate time every day to prayer and worship, and make sure you join a strong fellowship that encourages your walk with the Lord. When you're close to Him, you will not be easily swayed by the influences of this world and the voices of the age.

It's hard to lie to me about my dear wife, Kelly. On almost any subject, I can tell you exactly what her answer or preference would be. Whether it is some advice she gave, how she reacted to a situation, or even what she said about a situation, I can instantly recognize and reject something that is outside her character. I know her.

In the same way, we can know God. We can become so familiar with His ways that when we're confronted with a new idea, we'll instantly know whether He would approve. If someone approaches us with some new understanding of a scripture or doctrine, we can recognize right away whether it fits with His character. All the foolish and misguided ideas that have floated throughout the church, and every single central tenet of progressive

Christianity, would be immediately rejected if Christians were spending enough time with God and His Word, to know Him that well.

The prodigal returned and was immediately pulled close by the father. What a beautiful picture of God's grace! Those who have strayed into wokeism, progressive Christianity, Christless conservatism, or any other misrepresentation of the gospel have reason to hope. God is kind-hearted and long-suffering to restore the penitent to a right relationship with Him. In fact, He is overjoyed at the idea!

The prodigal's father was not satisfied with having his son return to the house. He wanted him restored to the position that was always his. He did not set about punishing, scolding, or embarrassing the repentant boy. Instead, he ordered the servants into action. Immediately, the estate was full of people moving about, preparing for a great celebration. The returning son, presumed dead, was alive! How much more must God rejoice when Christians, leaders, and churches return to Him?

You and I are alive at a very exciting time in the church. For decades there has been an encroachment of bad ideas into much of the church world. Many of us were either browbeaten into silence or ostracized away from influence. That is all changing. No longer do those ideas control the ability to platform weak voices while censoring the brave. Technology has made connections easier than ever. Truth speakers are being discovered. Those who may have been bullied away from standing strong are now calling the church back to righteousness, and they cannot be stopped. People are flocking to bold churches, and bold Christians are inspiring fellow believers to stand strong. The dead church has come alive—and that is a great reason to celebrate!

The prodigal's return was marked by celebration, but we also see the father take other significant actions. These actions can give some insight into what God is doing in this moment of voices in the church rising, this great return to righteousness. Heaven celebrates that so many leaders are now rejecting the cultural drift and fearful silence that has plagued us. But this is not all. We are also being given a mandate to fulfill our divine purpose.

In the story of the prodigal, the father sent for a new robe to be brought and his son to be clothed in it. Time in the far country and hours spent with the pigs left the son unfit to attend a celebration at the father's house. As part of his restoration, he was required to lay off the old and put on the new. In a spiritual sense, we see this in the life of a believer at salvation. As they begin to follow Christ and live out the new birth, they turn away from old habits, ideas, and ways of doing life as they grow in their faith and become more like Jesus.

As the church steps fully into its role for the hour, Christians must be committed to shedding the effects of the filth around us. Media, entertainment, and deceived influencers have poured lies into our eyes and ears. So many social contagions have invaded our thoughts, so much so that many believers have a difficult time determining where pop psychology ends and God's truth begins. Walking out the Father's will is going to require putting on the Father's thoughts.

Being clothed in righteousness is not an abstract concept. The armor of God is more than a poetic representation. We must intentionally lay off the ideology of the world and put on God's ways. We must lay down self-will and put on His will. We must rightly discern the things culture has attempted to ingrain in us and put on the mind of God.

This is straightforward, but it is not easy. The world tells us all sorts of things that are not in alignment with God's Word. Sometimes even Scripture or Christian principle is used as a method of pushing us toward wrong conclusions. Prayerfully, we can see it happening, reject wrong, and embrace right. We must leave prodigal Christianity behind and put on the full truth of faithful, unembarrassed commitment to our loving Lord.

Walking out the Father's will is going to require putting on the Father's thoughts.

Prodigal Christianity says truth is relative. Unembarrassed Christianity says truth is knowable and absolute.

Prodigal Christianity says family is whatever you want it to be. Unembarrassed Christianity says a husband and wife raising their children together is the basis of family.

Prodigal Christianity says gender roles are antiquated and oppressive. Unembarrassed Christianity says God created male and female with unique roles that cannot be fulfilled by the other.

Prodigal Christianity says life in the womb is only as viable as the mother wants it to be. Unembarrassed

Christianity says life is precious from conception to natural death.

Prodigal Christianity says sexuality and gender are fluid. Unembarrassed Christianity says sex was created for married, heterosexual couples and is wrong in every other context.

Prodigal Christianity says your sins are a result of the circumstances around you. Unembarrassed Christianity says every person is responsible for their own choices.

Prodigal Christianity says private property and wealth are evil and oppressive. Unembarrassed Christianity says Jesus supported private property and the commandments condemning theft (including forced charity) and covetousness.

Prodigal Christianity says the government should compel charity through social programs. Unembarrassed Christianity says believers should apply themselves in the marketplace, thrive, and then bless others from their abundance as an act of love and evangelism.

Prodigal Christianity says morality cannot be legislated, so Christians should stay out of government. Unembarrassed Christianity says God created family, government, and the church, and Christians should engage biblically in all three.

Prodigal Christianity says you will always be broken and bound by your choices and proclivities. Unembarrassed Christianity says that Jesus died to set you free and that you can be born again with new desires to make the right choices.

As Satan proved in the Garden of Eden, every

destructive secular ideology is rooted in a lie about God and His principles. Our call to reject them is made even more difficult by the fact that we are bombarded daily with indoctrination, both explicit and subliminal. When you choose what to watch or listen to, you may be careful to avoid certain things like nudity, violence, or foul language. That's great, but even the most seemingly innocent entertainment is often filled with subtle messaging that is antithetical to our moral values.

We must be prepared to resist falsehood by knowing the truth. We must also help defend our families against Satan's lies by being intentional about knowing what our children are consuming. Additionally, we should hold regular conversations with our children, and couples should do the same with each other. It is not enough to avoid the pigpen; we must consciously put on the Father's garments, take every thought captive, cast out wicked imagination, and have a ready defense for our beliefs and worldview.

RESTORED TO SPEAK WITH AUTHORITY

The returning son was also given a ring. This is widely believed to have been a ring that bore the family signet. In giving him the ring, the father restored his son's authority to make decisions and speak on behalf of the household. The son had either left his ring behind or squandered it in the far country, but now he was being given the rights and responsibilities of sonship once again.

The prodigal church is full of Christians who have abandoned or wasted their God-given authority. Some lost their witness when they got caught up in virtue signaling the values of the world. Others bought into the lie that the church has no business influencing the world. Thank God this is changing. We are in a moment when voices are rising to speak truth with God-given authority. The church is being blessed with those who no longer run from their God-given roles.

We see this in a return to bold preaching. Elders, pastors, and teachers are given explicit instruction in the New Testament. They have the duty to rightly divide the Word and feed the flock. Unembarrassed leaders are answering their call and boldly applying Scripture to every area of life, including the difficult, controversial topics that many avoid. They are also increasingly willing to confront false teaching and teachers.

Pastors, as Christ's undershepherds, are tasked with protecting the sheep. The church's infatuation with nice-first theology gave the wolves free rein, and the results are ugly. Unembarrassed pastors have had enough. They are standing up and declaring when they see danger. They are willing to be specific regarding the teachings that should be avoided and are even calling out false teaching by name. They recognize that their duty is always to protect the church by rebuking false teaching before it can take root and cause harmful division among God's people.

Unembarrassed believers are engaging in evangelism at new levels. They recognize that the only hope for the lost and dying is to encounter and embrace the radical saving grace of Jesus. They are shaking off the prodigal-church lies of universal salvation and the abuse of God's grace. They refuse to be fooled by the lie that spreading the gospel is imperial and oppressive. They know that a relationship with Jesus means liberty, freedom, and fullness of life. They refuse to stop until all have heard the good news of Christ's love and forgiveness.

When you walk into a church led by unembarrassed leaders, you'll hear about discipleship groups, classes, and workshops that deal with every area of the believer's life. Discipleship is at the center of these fellowships. They know that a conversion experience is only the beginning of a believer's journey. There is also a tangible belief that the church is the best place for people to learn how to raise children, run a business, handle their finances, recover from past hurts, overcome addiction, and live a fulfilled life that brings glory to God. They are not afraid to address every area of discipleship. They are not taking a back seat to secular programs and institutions, because they know that God's wisdom is always supreme.

Much has been said about the increase in Christians being vocal regarding the cultural and political issues of the day. Unembarrassed Christians are not afraid to address any of these issues and to do so publicly. They know that our true moral authority is not a political party or a DC think tank but the Word of God. They are not afraid to develop relationships with political or community leaders because they know that God's ways are best for any city, state, or nation.

Unembarrassed churches actively look for ways to support Christians in carrying their Christian principles into the marketplace and into places of authority. They know that a city filled with Christian business owners will be blessed because righteousness exalts a nation. They encourage Christians to run for office because they believe the Bible when it says that "the people rejoice" when the righteous "are in authority" (Prov. 29:2, NLT).

If you take a moment and look around, you are going to find that unembarrassed Christians are showing up, even in unexpected places. As I travel, I meet bold, Spirit-filled, biblical believers in places that are far beyond the typical Bible Belt areas of the nation. Wherever darkness has reigned and the prodigal church has followed from a distance, God is raising up the unembarrassed to shine His light.

Your family, your town, your church, your nation, and your world need you to live as an unembarrassed Christian.

A robe, a ring, and new shoes. The father handed the returning youth all he needed to walk out the next steps as a fully restored son. Today, God is giving the Western church an opportunity to repent of prodigal Christianity and walk in the fullness of our calling. God is calling churches, leaders, and everyday believers. God is calling you!

Your family, your town, your church, your nation, and your world need you to live and thrive as an unembarrassed Christian. Do not leave it to the pastors or your favorite YouTube Bible teacher. It's time for you to stand up, walk boldly, and speak clearly and faithfully in accordance with God's truth.

Remember, Peter had been given hope. His usefulness to God did not end at his denial. Beyond his failure, God would use him to strengthen the others. It would not be easy, but God would empower him for the job.

You may look back at your life and recognize areas in which you've been a prodigal Christian. You may have allowed terrible ideology to influence your thinking. You may have been afraid to push back as people you love were deceived by Satan. The cultural pressure may have subtly pulled you away from God's truth. You might be looking around and recognizing that something stinks about your thinking and living. I have good news. You have a reason for hope. Every prodigal does.

God is calling you to walk close to Him again. Throw off worldly thinking, and put on righteousness. Stand in authority on His Word. It won't always be easy, but if Peter could recover, with God's help, so will you. Walk in truth and watch what God does.

It is time to commit to being unembarrassed.

Bold speech should be matched with bold action. Scan the QR code or visit bit.ly/4mBII9B to join people around the United States in impacting the lives of children each Christmas. This community began in 2011. It's flourishing because thousands of bold voices mobilize together. Join the movement.

Chapter 8

EMPOWERED FAITH

"In the last days," God says, "I will pour out my Spirit upon all people. Your sons and daughters will prophesy. Your young men will see visions, and your old men will dream dreams."
—ACTS 2:17, NLT

H E COULD NOT explain how, but it felt different this time. He knew what it was to be emotional, which had gotten him into trouble many times. This was not that. He sometimes had this nagging feeling that he had to act because no one else was going to do whatever needed to be done. He had known that feeling since childhood. This was not that either. He felt no anxiousness to make something happen, and he was not reacting in the heat of the moment. This was something new and different altogether.

The crowd had grown to the point where there was almost no way through. He looked into the faces of people whose clothing gave them away as being from far-off places. Somehow, excitedly explaining all that had happened upstairs, he had spoken to several of them. It had not even occurred to him that they did not share a common language. Miraculously, they understood what he was saying. The other disciples had done the same. Word was spreading quickly that something strange was happening.

"They are drunk," called a voice from the crowd.

"I do not think so," came a reply. "I know full well that they are all speaking languages they would never know."

Looking across the crowd, Peter saw a sea of humanity bearing every shade of skin color, hailing from every nation in the region. Something in him stirred. He was not angry at their accusation of him and his companions being drunkards. Instead, he was moved with love for them. They were ignorant of the truth, a truth he knew would change their lives. They needed to hear it. He would tell them.

Wait, was he doing the same thing again? Was this another one of his impulses? Should he just wait? No, this was the moment. This was what Jesus had been talking about. He stepped up onto a stairway so he could be heard over the crowd and took a deep breath.

"Men of Judea and all who dwell in Jerusalem, let this be known to you, and give ear to my words" (Acts 2:14, ESV).

The people began to turn toward him. He felt a supporting hand on his shoulder. His fellow disciples gathered to stand with him. He felt his mind become clear, and the perfect wording began to form as he spoke.

"These people are not drunk, as you suppose, since it

is only the third hour of the day. But this is what was uttered..." (vv. 15–16, ESV).

Recitation had not always been his strong point. He could tell you every task and tool on a fishing vessel. He could recall exactly how long one would need to row and in which direction, depending on the weather, to catch the most fish on any given day out on Lake Tiberias. However, he was never really a man of books. No matter—the words of the prophet rolled off his tongue with the ease of the teachers reading directly from the scrolls in the synagogue.

The gathered crowd now gave him their full attention. Many of them knew of the prophecies, but they had not heard them spoken of so clearly—and certainly not in a place like this or by such a man. He had no phylacteries, no robes of the educated teachers, but his words seemed to strike directly in the softest part of each listener's heart.

He was now speaking of Jesus. This was a subject he knew well. Gone was the shame of his denials. His fear was nowhere to be found. A new and unfamiliar courage seemed to make him taller and bolder.

"You crucified Him"—he pointed at the crowd—"God raised Him up!"

Some gasped, and others began to weep. Peter continued to speak, laying out a perfect case for belief in Christ. Through the empowerment of the Holy Spirit, the fisherman wove a masterful sermon. He quoted Joel and David. He testified of the resurrection. With the crowd, including officers of Rome, listening in, he lifted his voice with a moral, spiritual, religious, and political declaration that would shake the world.

"Let all the house of Israel therefore know for certain that God has made him both Lord and Christ, this Jesus whom you crucified" (v. 36, ESV).

(For Peter's complete sermon and its effect on the crowd, see Acts 2:14–43.)

~

His words pierced hearts in the crowd, and they called out, wondering what to do. Peter responded with a bold imperative. He called on them to repent. He assured them of salvation if they would throw themselves on the mercy of the Lord Jesus Christ. When he was finished, three thousand souls were saved and baptized. What a day!

I've been part of some pretty big baptisms. I've baptized people in the ocean, pools, troughs, and baptisteries. Some days we baptized dozens and dozens of people, but I still have not had a 3,000-baptisms day. Yet. If each of the twelve disciples baptized an even number, that would be 250 baptisms each. I can assure you that is a spiritually rewarding but physically exhausting day.

THE BOLDNESS OF THE SPIRIT-FILLED LIFE

It's hard to believe that the same Peter who denied Jesus on the night of His arrest would then stand and declare that He was Lord and Christ. That statement would get you in trouble with both the religious crowd and the political crowd. In fact, there are few things that could be more dangerous for a person to declare. What had changed with Peter?

And he was not the only one who was radically different. The other disciples hadn't exactly been heroes the night Jesus was arrested. John had stayed close, standing at the foot of the cross during Christ's last moments. Beyond John there was very little to admire in the terrified disciples. They took cover during Jesus' ordeal. When He had risen from the dead, He found them hiding behind locked doors. Then when He sent them out to build His church, they seemed more concerned with Him establishing a temporal kingdom. They still did not fully grasp what the kingdom of God was all about. Yet there they were, standing alongside Peter, risking their lives for Jesus' sake. What had happened?

Peter and the rest of the disciples had undergone a drastic change. They had seen Jesus after the resurrection and witnessed His ascension to heaven, but this was more than a matter of changed logic. Jesus had sent them into Jerusalem to be empowered as His witnesses. That empowerment happened. They encountered the Holy Spirit. Their lives and the entire story of humanity would never be the same.

It would be easy for us to look at the story of Pentecost as some ethereal instance when the Holy Spirit moved and made people be something completely different from themselves. We could convince ourselves that this moment was so unique and outside the norm for the church that their boldness and the results were one-off happenings that are not to be expected in today's church. But an examination of the Scripture tells a different story.

The day of Pentecost, specifically the moment when Peter delivered that church-birthing sermon, offers a pattern for the modern church. In the days leading up to this moment, we can see parallels with our circumstances. In the actions of the disciples and the Jesus followers gathered with them, we find guidance for how we ought to navigate our lives and ministries. Just as there was a promised kingdom purpose for Peter after his denial, there is a God-ordained role for unembarrassed Christians as the church realigns with its call.

For us to be effective in our kingdom efforts, we must recognize the context in which we operate. Our context is not defined by the media, academics, or experts—including church experts. If we allow the terrain to be defined by the world, we will find ourselves making excuses for our ineffectiveness. Many labels can be placed on our current situation. We can call it postmodern, post-Christian, post-truth, and even post-church. Depending on how we define each of those terms, we could find a plethora of reasons to change our message.

By allowing secular experts to tell us what truth was, we gave up the most basic ground in sharing the gospel.

We have seen this in the Great Awokening (yes, that is the intentional spelling) of the church. By allowing secular experts to tell us what truth was, we gave up the most basic ground in sharing the gospel: that truth is absolute and that it can be known. By being convinced that we had moved beyond the church era, many settled for allowing the ungodly to control public discourse and discouraging Christians from seeking to hold positions of authority. You do not have to look far to see how disastrous this has been. Allowing the world to define context is costly.

Beyond the sociological and philosophical attempts to contextualize our present moment, there are also theological positions that have placed the church in a context that does not match reality. Our context is the same as that of the early church, even though we are separated by thousands of years. We are under orders to be about the business of sharing the gospel as Christ's ambassadors. The Great Commission is our mission.

Throughout the centuries, there have been many areas in which the church has engaged. We have seen the church in close relationship with governmental authorities, even as far as Christianity being the state religion. We have also seen the church persecuted and Christianity outlawed. However, our mission has always been the same: to see people changed by the power of Jesus Christ and be good citizens wherever we are. Sometimes that looks like resisting an evil government, and other times it looks like helping believers in their calling to serve in government. In either case our context is still the life-changing gospel of Jesus.

The church has always engaged in humanitarian activities. One rallying cry of those who wish to protect the legalized murder of children in the womb is that Christians are only pro-birth, not pro-life. These people have obviously not taken a look around to see the incredible number of hospitals, orphanages, and other charitable works built by the resources and efforts of Christ followers. They also fail to recognize that Christians are measurably the leaders in charitable and volunteer work. God's people have been doing good—good worth billions of dollars and changed lives—since before we were allowed to worship in public.

But for all the good the church has done, good works are not our primary mission. Good works are a tool by which people can open their eyes to a saving knowledge of Jesus. Yes, we feed the hungry, clothe the poor, house the needy, treat the sick, and so much more, but that is all secondary. Our primary context remains the call to see people changed through a relationship with Jesus as their Lord and Savior.

There is no telling how many souls could be reached if these Christians would only make the effort.

This reality, that the transforming gospel is our number one responsibility, has been missed by the compromised church. They have bought into progressive Christianity, liberation theology, and other unscriptural ideas that are more akin to Marxism than anything biblical Christians have ever believed. Their efforts center on changing the plight of man through "social justice," which has almost no concept of justice and is generally propagated using (and affirming) some pretty antisocial behavior. This has left them devoid of the only thing people really need from a church: a gospel that sets them free. It's no wonder that these churches are dying.

There are also those in the church who have developed a sense of escapism. To them the world is just a bad, sinful, scary place and there is nothing they can do about it. The second part is where they're wrong. The world is broken, but Jesus is the fixer of broken people. Nevertheless, they isolate themselves—like the last embassy workers in a fallen nation do, until the moment of their evacuation. There is no telling how many souls could be reached if these Christians would only make the effort.

Our context remains the same as that of the disciples at Pentecost. We await the return of our Lord Jesus Christ. Our responsibility is to carry out the Great Commission and bring souls into the kingdom. Knowing that we could not do this without His assistance, God is gracious to empower us for the task. The Holy Spirit working through us makes our efforts fruitful, gives us strength when we're weak, and emboldens us in the face of challenges. We are His unembarrassed, Spirit-empowered witnesses on earth.

The Holy Spirit's role in the life of the bold believer is often misunderstood. We live in a world that makes jokes about the anointing and moving of the Spirit on a person. Some of the worst offenders are in the church and among Christian entertainers and influencers. The unembarrassed Christian knows that the Holy Spirit is not to be dismissed or marginalized. It is His presence in us that empowers us for the task of sharing the gospel. Without Him we fail.

Knowing the necessity of the Holy Spirit in our lives, we must make His presence our priority. The disciples experienced the outpouring of the Holy Spirit, but they did not do so on their own terms. Not only were they operating within the context that Christ had laid out for them, but they were also walking in obedience to His command. Both are required for unembarrassed Christians to fulfill their call.

Christian faith works only when lived wholeheartedly. It simply isn't logical to make the claims we do about Christ and then follow Him in any half measure. We are not subscribers to a school of philosophy or adherents to the lifestyle advice of some guru. Our faith declares that Jesus is Lord. It logically follows that our service to Him will involve unreserved conformance to His commands. The unembarrassed Christian is not only bold enough to *speak* righteously but also brave enough to *serve* righteously.

In the days after Christ's ascension to heaven, the disciples had many options. They had families they likely had not seen regularly during their travels with Jesus. It would have been easy for them to return home. After all, they had put in their time. Surely God would understand that they were just making up for lost time. Someone else could go wait in Jerusalem.

Some of them were businessmen. While they had traveled with Jesus, there had been many lost opportunities. Now that He had ascended, how could they be expected to make a living? Yes, He had said they were to be His witnesses, but had they not already made many sacrifices? It was well past time to earn some income and enjoy life.

There may have been the temptation to start their own itinerant ministries. They had witnessed the resurrection. They knew He was who He said He was. No time could be wasted in "waiting for power." (See Acts 1:4–5, 8.) With their story people would be sure to believe. Who could be upset with such a noble cause as not delaying the sharing of the gospel?

There was more. Even if they wanted to do what He said, was it really wise? Jerusalem was full of the people who had crucified Him. Yes, the disciples and others had seen Him alive, but certainly there were many who didn't believe them. A better course would be to get far from the city. Maybe go back to Capernaum; there had been a lot of fruitful ministries there.

The reasons to neglect the Upper Room were as diverse as the group itself. You might say they had as many reasons not to obey Him as we do. Have you ever noticed how easy it is to come up with excuses for why we're not following His commands? We've become quite skilled at it. We're also talented at making our disobedience seem like it's for the best of reasons, the kind of reasons that God certainly would understand.

The believers' empowerment did not happen until they obeyed His instructions.

OBEDIENCE OPENS THE DOOR TO POWER

But the believers' empowerment did not happen until they obeyed His instructions. We cannot expect to experience His presence in our efforts when we're living in rebellion to His ways. It is certainly true that secular and even ungodly people can gather fame, influence, and wealth through speaking boldly about the issues of the day (especially when there is a lack of bold Christian voices). Some may even speak things in alignment with Christian principles and achieve much success for themselves and their platforms. However, this is not our goal.

Remember, our context is to operate under His command. We are not simply skilled in cursing the darkness. The secular commentator can fulfill that role quite well. Our job is to bring the transcendent light of the gospel into those dark places. We are not only in the business of pointing out that society is filled with people who have been chained to incredibly bad ideologies. You do not have to be a Christian to see that. Our job is bigger. We come declaring there is freedom and transformation in Jesus.

The purpose of our boldness is not self-serving. We may be blessed with platforms and influence, even providentially granted favor with men and governments. Yet none of these things is an end unto itself. They are all tools for our greatest purpose: bringing the gospel into every situation, setting, and arena of life. For this the Holy Spirit's empowerment is nonnegotiable.

As the disciples walked in obedience, they positioned themselves for an encounter with God. The same happens in our lives. As we begin to walk closely with Him, spend time in the Bible, participate in personal times of worship, and associate with a strong fellowship of believers, we make ourselves available for God encounters. Out of those comes empowerment to live as unembarrassed believers.

This is not to say that every bold believer starts from a powerful spiritual position. Some Christians are almost forced into their moment of bravery. They may take a small step like posting a Bible verse in their cubicle or praying over their lunch. Or they may do something straightforward like speaking up about their child being indoctrinated at school. This doesn't mean they spent three hours a day in personal devotions or were considered the best Christian in their church. It could be that their moment of boldness found them.

When that happens, God's grace is so amazing. He steps into the situation and helps us navigate from a strength far beyond our own spirituality. If you ever find yourself in one of those moments, the next step is to begin to be bold. Hell hates boldness. The best thing you can do is prepare for counterattack. Pray early and often. Spend quality time in the Word. Surround yourself with unembarrassed believers who will stand with you.

Courage has a way of inspiring others. When Peter rose to speak at Pentecost, the Scripture tells us that he stood with the other disciples. They stood together, unified in their boldness. Their standing helped him speak, and his speaking helped them stand. Boldness begets boldness, and there is nothing better than having bold brothers and sisters to stand with you.

The weekend after the story of my city council prayer had taken off, we were under fire. My family had been doxed, we were receiving threats, and new public or legal attacks seemed to be coming daily. For a pastor one thing never changes: Sunday is coming. That Sunday I was prepared to preach but really didn't know what the day was going to look like. Were there going to be protesters? Would the service be disrupted? Should I expect a media circus? Anything could happen. So I prayed for God to be with us and guide us through the moment for His glory. Then my phone rang.

"I'm coming to sit with you today, Travis." The voice on the other end was a friend and pastor, Nathaniel Carson, in our town.

Nathaniel led an incredible church and had his own ministry to oversee that morning, but he knew we were under attack. So on a Sunday morning, he came to sit at Pathway Church while I preached. It was an amazing moment of brotherhood. Boldness and boldness coming together.

One pastor made a bold decision to stand with another pastor who prayed a bold prayer. Out of that, something special was birthed in Mobile. We joined with other pastors in our city to form the Mobile Bay Pastors. Together that group saw positive change in our city. The extreme leftists pushing trans ideology on our kids were pushed back, and our city government even fired their LGBTQ liaisons. Two bold pastors became more than fifty bold pastors, and Mobile became the first city in America to intentionally take actions that lowered its score with the extremist Human Rights Campaign. As Peter stood with the disciples, we stood together. Unembarrassed believers saw incredible results shake their cities.

When you decide to be bold, others will follow. When you decide to walk faithfully in front of your family, don't be surprised when your spouse or children begin to make bold decisions too. When you speak up for truth in your church, others are likely to join you, emboldened by your faith. On the job, at school, at your kid's sports club, or with your friends, when you are unembarrassed, others will follow.

Peter and the other disciples saw incredible things on the day of Pentecost. We saw amazing things in Mobile. Across the United States, unembarrassed believers are seeing the faithfulness of God work great results. There is no reason you should not experience the same thing. Remember our context, walk in obedience, expect the Spirit's empowerment, and get ready for good results. Courageous faith becomes contagious faith. Then the unembarrassed change the world.

Scan the QR code or visit bit.ly/46s3fc5 to join one of my Jesus Revolution Kids, Dallas Davis, and me for a discussion about sharing your faith.

Chapter 9

COURAGEOUS, CONTAGIOUS FAITH

Then Philip ran up to the chariot and heard the man reading Isaiah the prophet. "Do you under-stand what you are reading?" Philip asked. "How can I," he said, "unless someone explains it to me?" So he invited Philip to come up and sit with him.
—ACTS 8:30–31

THE EXPONENTIAL GROWTH of the early church was an odds-defying testament to the empowerment of the Holy Spirit working through bold believers. Most new religious sects die out quickly. Those that manage to grow most often do so by the power of the sword, pushing their agenda forward through violence. Christianity survived the arrest and execution of its founder; the imprisonment, torture, and killing of its early members; and an entire loss of status and wealth by those who chose to follow its teachings. Not only did it survive; it grew.

The day of Pentecost planted the seeds of a movement that would take the world by storm. As people left the city and returned to their homes, they took the gospel with them. Each of them, and each person with whom they shared the gospel, was the direct beneficiary of one man's courageous moment. Peter stood and declared the truth, a truth that would eventually cost him his life. They found their way into the kingdom on a path paved by his bravery.

We will not always see the results of being bold for God; faithfulness is a reward in and of itself.

Peter's willingness to stand, and the camaraderie of his fellow disciples standing with him, is inspirational to us all. We will not always see the results of being bold for God; it could be years or even decades before the effects of one person's obedience are fully realized. You may never become aware in this life of the effect your faithfulness has on others. Faithfulness is a reward in and of itself. Just as one plants and another waters, the results may come long after your season—but they will come.

Although the full consequences of our actions may not be realized quickly, the early church does reveal a pattern of human behavior each of us can see in our own lives. Movements begin with one person who is willing to take a step. Others may have considered the same action; they may see the same need or have identified the same problem but don't know what to do about it. Then one person steps up, and others are encouraged to join in. Courage is contagious.

You never really know who around you simply needs a nudge to step forward and walk in boldness. In Mobile so many amazing leaders were disturbed over the direction of our city. None of them felt it was right that the city was funding sexualized entertainment with children as its target. They all agreed that something must be done. It took an attack on one of us to stir the boldness within all of us. Together we stood, encouraged by one another, and we saw great things happen.

The early church benefited greatly from the courage of its leaders. You would never have recognized the disciples as the same ones who had fled Gethsemane during the arrest of Jesus. They had come a long way since hiding behind closed doors in fear for their lives. These did not seem like the same men; something had changed. They had encountered the resurrected Savior. They had been empowered by the Holy Spirit. They were unembarrassed, unafraid, and courageously confident that God was with them in everything they did.

It's good for us to revisit the Book of Acts and see what these empowered believers were like. They repeatedly took actions that were risky. They challenged norms, pushed back against government oppression, and even risked their lives for the sake of the gospel. They were not just risking being uninvited from the family reunion or being blocked on social media. Their boldness could mean prison, even death. Their choices were not easy, but they chose boldness, and God repeatedly blessed their decisions.

Unembarrassed Christianity has been the central thread running through church history since the moment Peter delivered the gospel on the day of Pentecost. For most of us, it's hard to imagine the immense pressure the disciples were under that day. The crowd was full of diverse people from all over the region. The authorities had already crucified Jesus and would certainly not want any unrest to be stirred among the multitudes. The temple rulers had a vested interest in shutting down the followers of Jesus. They had already offered bribes to cover up the resurrection and eventually would send representatives to hunt down those in the synagogues who followed Him. The last thing they needed was for the populace to be stirred up. There was no limit to what they would do to stop it.

Peter had every reason to simply shut up and try to go back to his life as a fisherman. And he was not the only one who could have chosen a much easier path. No one could have blamed the other disciples if they had tried to silence him or if they had just melted back when the crowd began to gather. Instead, their boldness inspired them to stand with him as Christ was declared Lord and Savior. Out of this, three thousand were converted, baptized, and sent to their hometowns as the foundation of the church.

Inspired by the uncompromising witness of the apostles, early followers of Christ set about sharing the gospel. The first chapters of Acts tell the story of people who dedicated their lives to their faith, shared in helping one another, and gathered frequently to grow together. This was not without challenges. Early Christians risked relationships and their place in the community by joining with the followers of "the Way" (Acts 9:2, NKJV).

As more Jews began to follow the apostles' teaching regarding Jesus, the pressure was building in their synagogues and with the temple authorities. This new sect was threatening to tear down their authority. Killing Jesus should have been the end of them, but somehow they had persevered. As the religious leaders escalated their efforts to shut down the Christ followers, one preacher drew their attention.

A young man named Stephen had been having incredible success in his efforts. His notoriety was aided by God confirming his ministry through wonders and signs. To make matters worse, when he was confronted, Stephen responded with such wisdom that the arguments of his opponents fell far short of convincing the people to reject his teaching. So they plotted against him, conspiring to charge him falsely with blasphemy.

At this point Stephen had a choice to make. With his life on the line, he could have begged for their forgiveness and said he misspoke. He could have accepted their demands to silence his preaching. Instead, in an echo of Peter on Pentecost, Stephen delivered a bold sermon that declared Jesus was Messiah and Lord. His words so incensed the hearers that they stoned him to death. The church had its first martyr—one of the empowered witnesses Christ had told them they would be. The rulers of the day killed Stephen, but they were too late to stop his contagious courage from spreading.

The church leaders scattered throughout the region, in God's providential plan to enable the spread of the gospel. Among them was Philip, whose ministry bore much fruit. He was preaching in Samaria and saw great crowds of people gathering to hear and to see the signs that confirmed his anointing. Then the Lord unexpectedly led him from that place to an encounter that would challenge his trust.

COURAGE IN THE DESERT ROAD ENCOUNTER

Having been sent by God to a road through the desert, Philip encountered the chariot of an Ethiopian official who was returning from a trip to worship in Jerusalem. The Holy Spirit moved Philip to engage with the official, who was reading the writings of Isaiah as he rode. Speaking to a government official was not an easy ask for the apostle. What if this man reported him to the authorities? What if he was arrested and exchanged with the authorities in Jerusalem as part of some political maneuver?

The same Holy Spirit empowerment that strengthened Peter on Pentecost was present in Philip. He did not shrink back from the moment. At great risk to himself, Philip led the official through the Scriptures and shared the gospel. Instead of rebuking him or demanding his arrest, the official asked to be baptized! Most scholars believe this official returned to Ethiopia and shared the good news of Jesus with his countrymen. Philip's courage proved contagious indeed.

Peter's courage led to thousands being saved. Philip's led to one. In each case, God's hand was working through willing believers who were unafraid to share the good news. We never know the context in which God will prompt us to be courageous. It might mean speaking truth before a group at work or even in front of a crowd, or it could be as simple as sharing the gospel one-on-one with a hungry soul. We never know just how impactful that moment of courage may be.

Being an unembarrassed Christian will sometimes put us in uncomfortable positions. It was never in my plans for my family to bear the assaults of an online mob, but God knew that our city needed me to do exactly what He had led me to do. It certainly would be easier for us all to silence our witness and avoid anything that could be difficult, but cowardice never advances the kingdom.

God's hand works through willing believers who are unafraid to share the good news.

The ninth chapter of Acts introduces us to a man who had to decide between comfort and calling. Ananias was a disciple of Christ who lived in Damascus. The believers there were next on the target list of Saul, who had overseen the killing of Stephen and had been tasked with cleansing the synagogues of all the Jesus followers. He had the authority to do whatever was necessary to make sure that Judaism was spared from these people he believed to be blasphemous heretics.

Saul had an encounter on the road to Damascus, but

Ananias did not know this. When the Lord told Ananias to go and pray for Saul, you can imagine the fear that must have come over him. The church in Damascus had probably been preparing to avoid Saul, but now God was telling him to go and pray for the man? This made no sense at all.

What would you have done in that moment? It would have been a struggle for most of us. We would have thought about our families, our freedom, and of course our lives. Ananias struggled for a moment in his conversation with God. Ultimately, he was convinced that he had heard from the Lord and went to where Saul was staying. He risked his life and changed church history, all in the same bold moment.

The New Testament overflows with moments when courageous faith proved to be contagious faith.

That moment of bravery led to the ministry that would plant churches throughout the known world and give us the majority of our New Testament. Through Saul—later renamed Paul—we would receive life-changing doctrinal writing and instruction for the church. There is no way it was easy for Ananias to meet with Saul. He may have questioned himself all the way there, but he chose bold faith—and helped change the world.

Have you ever had God deal with you about sharing the gospel with someone? You may have struggled over how difficult it would be. Be careful that you do not resist what God wants to do through you. You never know what other work God has already been doing in someone's heart. You may think that person would never receive the gospel, but if God is leading you, it's always time to be unembarrassed in obedience. You never know what could come of that one interaction.

The New Testament overflows with moments when courageous faith proved to be contagious faith. From Peter making the decision to share the gospel with the household of Cornelius to Paul sharing the gospel with a businesswoman along the banks of a river to a jailer calling out for salvation after he thought faithful apostles had escaped his prison, bold faith made for big results, and the kingdom grew. The early disciples were willing to risk everything to tell people about Jesus. They confronted mobs, withstood natural dangers, pressed for their rights in the courts, and were ostracized by their own friends and families. They were unembarrassed, and their contagious courage set the stage for all Christian history.

There have certainly been places and moments being a Christian was easier than others. Many of us have no idea what it is to truly suffer for the sake of the gospel. It's hard for us to understand that we are standing on the shoulders of men and women who often had nothing other than their courageous faith. The perils of discipleship did not end when the last of the New Testament was penned. For centuries the exclusive catalyst for the church's growth was courageous faith.

How much courage would it take for a person to return to a land from which they had escaped slavery in order to share Christ? That is what Patrick, the fifth-century church father, did. Not only were the Irish his former captors, but they were also deeply rooted in paganism. Bringing them the gospel would prove to be a difficult and dangerous task. He endured rejection, threats, and heavy opposition, both spiritual and physical. Despite being beaten, having his belongings stolen, and being threatened with execution, Patrick never gave up.

Eventually, he would see thousands baptized and is today given credit for Christianizing Ireland. Recently, I was blessed to spend time there, walk where he walked, and visit the town where his first missionary work took place. You cannot travel the country without finding abundant evidence of the work one unembarrassed believer did for the kingdom.

Patrick returned to his captors because God led him to do so. Are you bold enough to carry the gospel to people who have wronged you? When you are resisted, will you persist in gracefully, lovingly sharing the gospel? If you find yourself being hated for the truth, will you still tell it? Patrick did, and a nation was changed.

Shining the light of Jesus into the darkness of pagan bondage made for some incredible opportunities for boldness. A few centuries after Patrick took the gospel to Ireland, a man named Boniface traveled into Germania. After a few years of ministry efforts, he found himself in a moment that would test his devotion and challenge him to courageous faith.

TAKING THE AXE TO IDOLS

In the region where he had been sent to minister, Boniface came upon a tree known as the Donar's Oak (some call it Jupiter's Oak or Thor's Oak). The tree was believed to be sacred to the pagan gods. Boniface was not about to have Christian ministry overshadowed by pagan beliefs, so he decided to take drastic action. He grabbed an axe and went to cut down the oak. This was no small choice. The people could react by seizing him for attacking their sacred tree. He could be forced to flee or even be killed by those angered at his actions.

Boniface was not deterred. As the pagan crowd looked on, he hewed away at the mighty trunk. There are many stories regarding this moment. Some say that a strong wind came along and aided his efforts. Other accounts do not mention the wind, but they all agree on one thing: Boniface cut down the sacred tree. The crowd was astonished that their gods would allow him to get away with such a thing. When the missionary was not struck down by the pagan gods, the people became open to his message.

The courageous faith shown by Boniface proved to be contagious. People in the region began to respond to Jesus Christ. Many were converted, and Christian churches and monasteries were built across the land. Boniface's own church was built from the wood of the felled oak, a testament to the power of unembarrassed faith.

Boniface had no way of knowing what would happen when he wielded his axe against that tree. More than doing the work of a forester, he was waging war on constructs and ideologies. It wouldn't have been at all surprising if the day had ended with him a dead man, killed by the violent reaction of the pagan worshippers. Their reaction was of little consequence to him; he saw a symbol of their oppression and destroyed it. With its fall, down came the hold pagan darkness had on the souls of the men and women in that region.

Your world probably doesn't have any sacred oaks in it. No one is likely to believe pagan gods are waiting to strike you down for destroying their favorite tree. The idols of this age are not trees but ideas. Bad ideas. Many of us have fallen silent in the face of terrible ideologies that have been made sacred by our fallen world. The cost for speaking about things like sexual orientation and gender identity can be monumental. Refusing to bend the knee to the LGBTQ activists can result in losing your business, your friends, your job, and even your freedom. Even in developed Western nations, a simple action like sharing a Bible verse on your social media can result in being viciously slandered or canceled.

We were once a God-trusting nation that believed in prayer, involving Him in most public activities. Now we've seen followers of Christ lose their jobs because they dared to kneel for a silent prayer in public. Businesses face constant threats to make sure they signal support for the leftist ideas of the day, or else they could be boycotted, sued, or even burned to the ground. Marxist ideology has led to families being surrounded by hostile mobs demanding they join in reciting chants or posture their support. While we may not see literal trees, we are constantly navigating a world of sacred-oak ideas.

Are you willing to speak the truth on difficult subjects? When the conversation comes up at your job, will you refuse to bow? If you are threatened with being fired if you don't affirm someone's confused gender ideations, will you stand strong? What about when they send home a pride patch to sew on your child's sport uniform? Are you unembarrassed? Do you have the kind of courage that can be contagious?

You could spend countless hours reading the stories of courageous saints who changed the world through their boldness to follow Jesus: William Carey and his reliance on God as his wife's mental health deteriorated, Corrie ten Boom and her family hiding Jews from the Nazis, George Müller's trust in God's daily provision, Brother Andrew risking his life as God's smuggler, and thousands of other examples can be found. Jesus is our foundation, the Holy Spirit is our empowerment, and the bravery of unembarrassed believers is our testimony.

And courageous faith is not a thing of the past. Bold Christianity is not some bygone era over which we can wax nostalgic. Today, around the world, brothers and sisters are standing strong in the face of extreme difficulty. Missionaries take great risks to share the gospel. Christians face a barrage of lawsuits, public derision, and brutal attacks because they stand for biblical values. Faithful believers are ostracized by the very churches they helped build. Followers of Jesus are estranged from their families because they will not compromise. The price of boldness can be high, but no cost will ever outweigh the blessings of staying close to Jesus. He has overcome the world.

God is honoring the unembarrassed. Faithful churches are growing. Bold ministries are experiencing revival. Small groups are filling with disciples who want to know

God and His Word better. Dads and moms are engaging
with their children as never before. Truth speakers are
finding platforms outside the control of the dying, compromised church. People are coming to Jesus and learning
that life in Christ changes everything. The once bound
are escaping the lies of a backslid church that affirmed
their sin; they are being called to repentance and experiencing *true* freedom.

A generation has arisen that is not afraid to lay the axe
to the idols of the day.

Revival is breaking out because the truth indeed sets
you free.

Courageous, contagious faith is still changing the
world.

Scan the QR code or visit bit.ly/
46Ki9cs to learn how to share your
(Un)Embarrassed of Jesus story.

Chapter 10

WORLD-CHANGING FAITH

*For God has not given us a spirit of fear, but of
power and of love and of a sound mind.*
—2 TIMOTHY 1:7, NKJV

IT HAD BEEN more than thirty years since that terrible
morning. He still thought about it from time to time,
that sunrise when the rooster's crow had signaled the
lowest point of his life. So much had changed since then.
There was no denying Jesus now. Peter's name was so
synonymous with the church that he could not get away
with it if he tried.

He had witnessed many incredible happenings. The
church had grown by unbelievable measures. His fellow
apostles now spanned the known world, carrying the
gospel to three continents. Their courage infected those
they won to Christ. Christians (the name that had been
given them) regularly withstood danger in the name of

Jesus. The more opposed and oppressed the church was, the more rapidly it grew.

The early church faced difficulty from every side. In its fledgling moments, converts were almost entirely of Jewish lineage. For them conversion meant defying their own religious leaders, being ostracized by their communities, and accepting a very different type of Savior than the militant Messiah for which they had hoped. Additionally, Christianity, with its message of salvation by faith, was a novel approach to righteousness for a people who had always relied on their works and the sacrificial system. Even so, thousands of Jews were finding salvation in Jesus Christ.

Peter himself had pioneered ministry to the Gentiles. His dream, and the ministry to the household of Cornelius that followed, was a milestone moment in the church. As Gentiles came to Christianity from their various polytheistic and pagan backgrounds, new challenges arose. Many had been steeped in worship and rituals that were as barbaric as they were empty. Following Christ could lead to a great loss of status, property, and even their lives. Despite the risk, Gentiles flooded into the growing body of believers.

For those deciding whether to become followers of the Way, there were other factors to consider. They would also be making an extremely direct political statement by placing their faith in Christ. There had never been a more politically charged statement than a first-century believer declaring, "Jesus is Lord."

They lived in a time when Caesar was "Lord," and not

in the base sense that is still used to refer to those with inherited titles. If you were in the Roman Empire, you were ruled by a man who was seen not only as emperor but also as a god—your god. It was expected that every citizen would offer worship to Caesar and revere him as a deity. For Christians this worship of man was untenable. For Rome their refusal was unforgivable.

Peter had himself been on the wrong side of the law, both Jewish and Roman. Before the denial, he had attempted to intervene in Christ's arrest. After his repentance and the day of Pentecost, Peter's resistance to Rome no longer involved the sword, but he still found himself in some tough situations. He and John had been dragged before the Sanhedrin after healing a man in the name of Jesus. Refusing to be silenced, Peter and John had declared that they could speak only what they knew to be true.

It was not long before his bold unembarrassment landed Peter in hot water again. Refusing to stop talking about Jesus, he was arrested and returned to the Sanhedrin to answer for his insubordination. This time the order to stop preaching was accompanied by a flogging. But Peter and his companions would not be silenced. They continued to preach, and the church continued to grow.

Indeed, Peter had seen firsthand the power of contagious Christianity. He had been on the inside of a jail cell only to be delivered by an angel, then he saw the church grow even more. He had heard reports from around the known world as his fellow apostles also refused to bow to pressure, and people were being won to Christ as a result. Beatings, trials, shipwrecks, and jailings were all no match for unembarrassed Christians dedicated to sharing the gospel no matter the cost.

The pressure on the church boiled over under the reign of Nero. This wicked emperor, infamous for having his own mother killed, hated the Christians and wanted to see them wiped out. He seemed to enjoy making a show of his cruelty, often having believers killed in public and in exceedingly savage ways. He was known to have them fed to dogs or thrown to other beasts for the entertainment of the masses. Many were also said to have been fastened to poles or crosses and burned alive, used as torches to light his debauched revelries.

Becoming a Christian under Roman rule was no small thing. In today's world—where people are so afraid to be called a bigot that they refuse to speak truth on matters of morality, and where pulpits avoid biblical topics because they've been deemed political—it's hard to imagine the boldness required to live for Christ in the days of Rome. Yet thousands did, risking life and limb to follow and proclaim Jesus as Lord.

It was in this setting that Peter was a leader in the church. It's difficult to picture how a guy who melted under the questioning of a servant girl could ever have survived, but everything had changed for Peter. He had grown close to God; he had encountered and embraced the empowering of the Holy Spirit. Peter had reached the point Jesus told him would come: He had made it through the sifting and now was active in helping strengthen other believers.

The radical change in Peter from cowardice to courageous faith should give us all hope. Nobody gets it right
all the time. All of us have moments when fear pushes us
to be quiet, when self-preservation takes the lead over our
desire to honor God. Most of us, in our own ways, have
found ourselves on the wrong end of a Christ denial.

BOLDNESS IS A CHOICE

You probably have never fled a mob at the arrest of a
religious leader, but how many times have you retreated
from a conversation around the coffee machine at your
job? Maybe you never cursed someone when they asked
if you were a Christian, but have you ever tripped over
yourself trying to avoid answering a question the Bible
has clearly answered in a way the
world finds offensive? Have you ever
decided that your status with friends
was more important than being identified fully with Jesus Christ?

*None of us
has a perfect
track record
when it comes
to being bold.*

If you find any of those situations
familiar, you're not alone. None of
us has a perfect track record when
it comes to being bold. Sometimes our test comes in a
moment when we've been distracted, when there is distance between us and Jesus. Other times we have been
deceived by things that seemed close to the truth but
were far from God's truth. Then when we had the opportunity to speak truth, we were confused or wrong about
what God's truth really was. Thankfully, Peter's story is
a heartening reminder that your worst moments of fear

are not the end of your story. You have a choice. You can make the decision to start living boldly. Unabashedly, unashamedly Christian.

Peter's final act of boldness happened after things had taken a turn for the worse under Nero. A devastating fire had broken out in Rome, and Nero decided the Christians would be a good scapegoat. His cruelties reached a new height, and Peter's time to die drew close.

We do not know all the details about his death, except that most scholars agree he was executed during Nero's reign. Sources tell us that he was crucified, like the Savior he had once denied. We are also told that, because he felt himself unworthy to die in the same manner as Jesus, Peter asked to be crucified upside down. His request was granted. Somewhere in Rome, afraid no more, the unembarrassed apostle took his last breath and died for the One he had once denied.

Peter was not alone in dying the bold death of the unembarrassed. Before or soon after his death, several of the other disciples also came to violent ends. James the Greater was killed by the executioner's sword. Philip was scourged, imprisoned, and crucified. Matthew was killed by the sword, some say beheaded while standing at the altar of communion. Andrew was said to have preached for two days while dying on his cross. Paul was beheaded. James the Less was cast down from the temple and then clubbed to death.

Thomas, doubter no more, was pierced with a spear, dying with the same type of wound he had once examined in Christ's side. Bartholomew was flayed alive and then crucified. Jude was said to have been beaten to death or killed with arrows. Simon the Zealot was crucified. Matthias, the replacement for Judas, was stoned to death. Only John managed to die of natural causes after various tortures, including being thrown into boiling oil. While exiled to a remote and desolate island, he heeded the Word of the Lord and penned the Book of Revelation.

I cannot think of the price these unembarrassed men paid without being moved to tears. Their courage in the face of adversity is beyond remarkable. They changed the world and gave their lives because they followed Jesus so closely that not even the threat of death could make them turn away. As inspiring as their stories are, as otherworldly as their boldness seems, you and I are called to do the same.

God has not changed His call for us to be Christians who walk in the Spirit and overcome hardship for His glory.

It's easy to look at Peter or any of the other apostles and feel that they must have had some secret power. Surely, they must have been empowered by a different Holy Spirit than the Spirit who dwells in us. They took bold faithfulness to a level far beyond anything we can imagine. We would do well to remember that God, including God the Holy Spirit, does not change. We have not been empowered by some lesser version. God has not changed His call for us to be Christians who walk in the Spirit and overcome hardship for His glory.

How do we do it? How do we find the bravery that

these early followers of Christ lived and died by? How do we go from fearing social media heat to not being afraid to literally die for the gospel?

Choices.

By now you know I am not writing with some new approach that enables you to overcome fear and confusion through a set of previously undiscovered principles. I am doing quite the opposite. The answer the church needs is not a new one; it is the same solution that enabled the rapid spread of the good news in the days of the apostles. Christians simply need that one original ingredient: boldness.

The church needs the same solution that enabled the rapid spread of the good news in the days of the apostles: boldness.

Boldness is not inherited by blood. It cannot be bestowed through theoretical exploration. The only way to have the boldness of an unembarrassed Christian is to take the same steps the disciples took. I don't mean you need to buy a ticket to Israel and set about finding the Upper Room written about in Acts. I'm saying that these men did not arrive at boldness by nature of being who they were. They did bold things because they started making one bold choice at a time.

We celebrate the boldness of someone who is not afraid to call out sin in the public sphere or to declare righteousness in the face of impending compromise. We should. That kind of boldness is sorely needed. It edifies the church as well as the community. However, before you think your call to be bold begins by recognizing what's wrong in the church, in society, or in other believers, understand first that boldness begins a lot closer to home.

The call to boldness is personal. It begins with you. Are you bold enough to apply God's principles to every area of your life? It's great that you want to speak to government wickedness or call for righteousness in the church, but have you been bold enough to lead your family well? Are you bold in choosing your relationships? Are you boldly setting out to run your business with integrity, according to the principles in God's Word? Have you boldly put God first in your scheduling? Are you bold in living your daily life surrendered to the control and guidance of His Holy Spirit?

God has blessed me with many opportunities to share the truth in the face of opposition. It's been my honor to stand alongside some incredibly brave people who have made a mark as unembarrassed Christians. No matter how many times we stand together and no matter the difference we make in the world, my primary obligation for boldness is in my home.

I want to walk closely with Christ, to make sure there is no distance between us. This is not so I can be assured of His blessing on my ministry or so He will open up new opportunities or larger platforms. I need to be close to Him because I am called to bold leadership within the four walls of my home. Kelly needs an unembarrassed husband. Kourtney, Blake, and McKenna need an unembarrassed dad. My family deserves no less, and I want to do all I can to make sure they always have that.

The same is true in your world. There are people around you who need you to make those daily choices to stand strong in the faith. Your spouse, your children, your friends, and your fellow believers are all poised to be blessed by your decision to be a sold-out follower of Christ. Why would you give them anything less?

It would be a good idea to take pen and paper and list all those who count on you to be an unembarrassed Christian. It might be a much longer list than you originally thought. After all, your family, friends, and small group members all need you to be a bold believer, but it does not stop there. Your coworker who hasn't gone to church in years needs to see a bold witness on the job. The barista at your favorite coffee shop who has been questioning her atheism needs a bold Christian in her life. The baby who will be murdered in the womb needs bold Christians. The addicts in your city could use some bold Christians. Are you done writing yet? You may never be.

There is simply no other way to be a believer. If what we say about Jesus is true, then we have no choice but to be unembarrassed about following and obeying Him. It's completely illogical to attempt serving the King of the universe in any other manner. As you read this, you're not just deciding whether to be an unembarrassed Christian; you're deciding whether you will be a Christian at all. If He is Lord, unembarrassed is your only option. There is no other kind.

If you picked up this book because you're tired of the way things are in the world around you, I understand. If you feel it's time to stand up and start walking in courageous Christianity, I celebrate that work of God's Spirit in you. I'm excited at how blessed you will be when you see your courageous Christianity become contagious faith. It is amazing to walk out your faith without reservation.

Your journey begins with a choice.

Every morning, wake up and begin your day with a choice to be bold. It begins right there. The greatest battle for the believer is not with the world or even with the powers and principalities of spiritual conflict. Your greatest battle in living the unembarrassed Christian life will be against the fear that seeks to dissuade you from doing what's right.

Fear lies. Fear will whisper that standing for truth will cost you more than you can or want to pay. Fear will let you watch your children destroy their lives because you think speaking up will cost you your relationship with them. Embarrassment will have you worrying that people will think you're backward or strange if they find out you base your morality on God's Word. Fear has no boundaries that it will not cross and gives no warning when it attacks, but every single time, fear lies.

In 2 Timothy 1:7 (NKJV) Paul assures us, "God has not given us a spirit of fear, but of power and of love and of a sound mind." Paul didn't say we won't encounter fear. The fact that the origin of fear is being discussed lets us know that we can expect it to be present in the life of the believer. When Paul wrote to Timothy, he wanted the younger minister to understand that fear, though present, was to be directly countered by the gifts of God: power, love, and a sound mind. Being an unembarrassed Christian begins with deciding you will not be controlled by fear and doubt but will live confidently in the power, love, and sound thinking the Lord has given you.

If you want to change the world, you have to first change yourself. That begins with how you deal with fear. What are you afraid of? What fears are stopping you from going all in with your faith? Why have you been holding back on taking the next steps in your journey with God? You believe Jesus is who He said He is, so why are you not living every day as a courageous follower of Christ? The good news is, you can start now.

The most difficult task in leadership is leading yourself. The hardest struggle in being bold is with the old nature within. Once you get past yourself, there is very little that can stop you. We conquer ourselves, including our fear, by remembering that we are living sacrifices. This means we may have to endure some fires of hardship. If we can make it through without climbing down off the altar when the heat gets turned up, we will fulfill the charge of Romans 12:2: "Do not conform to the pattern of this world, but be transformed by the renewing of your mind." Rather than conforming to the world, we will walk according to God's call—transformed and strengthened by His Holy Spirit living within us.

Beginning with a look at Peter's denial, we've journeyed together through what happens when a person who followed from a distance makes the choice to be unembarrassed of Jesus. We can see the necessity for bold faith and recognize that there truly is no other way to set about following Him. So today, make a commitment to make and live bold choices. Choose to follow Him closely. Get into His Word every day. Pray early and often for the Holy Spirit's leading and power.

You may not always get it right, but refuse to quit. Our Father is quick to forgive. Be careful not to get distracted by all that's happening in the world around you. Guard yourself against the petty things and negative influences that could make you drift from Jesus. Find a solid group of fellow believers who can help you fight your battles. Make sure you have people in your life who will notice if you grow distant. Do whatever it takes to stay close to Him.

It is not likely that the world will suddenly become accepting of biblical Christianity. We may have moments of political reprieve or when oppositional voices seem to grow quiet, but those moments will pass. We are not of this world. Never forget that. You represent a kingdom that does not fit into the systems of man. Remember that representing a kingdom means you serve a king, and not just any king but the King of kings. There is only one way to represent Him: unembarrassed.

Bold faith begins in the heart of the follower, and it begins with a choice. One bold choice leads to more. Those choices begin to form a bold believer. Courageous faith is contagious faith. One bold believer becomes many. Great things begin to happen.

Together, following Jesus closely, unembarrassed Christians can change the world.

Bold, (Un)Embarrassed faith requires a community that keeps you growing and encouraged in the Scriptures. You should join a group like this in your church. If you are not in church or in a small group to grow in relationship and in scriptural maturity, scan the QR code or visit bit.ly/46Ztoz0 to find a group.

A PERSONAL INVITATION
FROM THE AUTHOR

GOD LOVES YOU deeply. His Word is filled with promises that reveal His desire to bring healing, hope, and abundant life to every area of your being—body, mind, and spirit. More than anything, He wants a personal relationship with you through His Son, Jesus Christ.

If you've never invited Jesus into your life, you can do so right now. It's not about religion—it's about a relationship with the One who knows you completely and loves you unconditionally. If you're ready to take that step, simply pray this prayer with a sincere heart:

Lord Jesus, I want to know You as my Savior and Lord. I confess and believe that You are the Son of God and that You died for my sins. I believe You rose from the dead and are alive today. Please forgive me for my sins. I invite You into my heart and my life. Make me new.

Help me walk with You, grow in Your love, and
live for You every day. In Jesus' name, amen.

To hear me personally pray with you to receive Christ, scan the QR code or visit bit.ly/4pKOKaV. I would be honored to guide you through the life-changing decision to accept Jesus and experience His love for yourself.

If you just prayed that prayer, you've made the most important decision of your life. All of heaven rejoices with you, and so do I! You are now a child of God, and your journey with Him has just begun. Please reach out to my publisher at pray4me@charismamedia.com if you accepted Jesus today or if this book has encouraged or impacted your life in any way. We'd love to celebrate with you and send you free materials to help strengthen your faith. We look forward to hearing from you!

NOTES

CHAPTER 1

1. Erica Thomas, "Pre-Council Prayer Continues in Mobile Despite Criticism of June 6 Prayer—'I Was Disturbed,'" 1819 News, June 20, 2023, https://1819news.com/news/item/pre-council-prayer-continues-in-mobile-despite-criticism-of-june-6-prayer.
2. Lewis Carroll, *Alice's Adventures in Wonderland* (London, 1865), chapter 1.

CHAPTER 2

1. Arnold Cole and Pamela Caudill Ovwigho, "Bible Engagement & Social Behavior: How Familiarity & Frequency of Contact with the Bible Affects One's Behavior," Center for Bible Engagement, presented at Tel Aviv University, April 2009, https://bttbfiles.com/web/docs/cbe/Bible_Engagement_and_Social_Behavior.pdf.

CHAPTER 6

1. Carrie Sheffield, "Why Generation Z Is Returning to God," *New York Post*, updated April 27, 2023, https://nypost.com/2023/04/26/why-generation-z-is-returning-to-religion/.
2. John Stonestreet and Shane Morris, "Young Men Are Returning to Church," Breakpoint, July 9, 2025, https://breakpoint.org/young-men-are-returning-to-church.
3. Lois M. Collins, "New Findings Challenge Pop Cultural Portrayals of Married Mothers," *Deseret News*, August 25, 2025, https://www.deseret.com/family/2025/08/25/married-mothers-happier-children-single-motherhood-study/.

4. "New Research on Church Attendance: Decline of Women or the Rise of Men?," Barna, October 7, 2025, https://www.barna.com/trends/church-attendance-women-men/; Christian Daily International, "Bible Reading Is Rising Among Younger Men, Surprising Researchers," *The Christian Post*, May 19, 2025, https://www.christianpost.com/news/bible-reading-is-rising-among-younger-men-surprising-researchers.html; "Gen Z, Gender, and Religion," Public Religion Research Institute, March 5, 2025, https://prri.org/spotlight/gen-z-gender-and-religion/.

ACKNOWLEDGMENTS

THE WORLD IS transformed by the bold and courageous who dare to step into the arena. There is no greater gift than the gospel courage of a child of God reaching out to someone who needs Jesus. To those fearless, obedient souls who share their faith unapologetically: Thank you for reshaping the world.

To my wife and best friend, Kelly: Your unwavering support through our shared steps of faith and acts of courage is a treasure. From urban Chicago to South Miami, from Asia to our daily pastoral work in Mobile, Alabama, you are a blessing to our family, our ministries, and me. For twenty-six years, we've been writing this book together. I love you.

To my parents, John Thomas Johnson and Anne Roberts Johnson: When Hurricane Andrew devastated your home, church, and city, your unashamed, bold ministry became my life's road map. You rebuilt your city and transformed my life. I love you both deeply for your lifelong devotion to Phillip and me. Dad, I miss you.

Kourtney, McKenna, and Blake: You deepen my love for Jesus and help me grasp the Father's love for me. I'm incredibly proud of you—warriors and world changers. Thanks for being in my book. The deal stands: Five dollars for a sermon shout-out. I'll pay up.

To Steve Strang, Chad Dunlap, Debbie Marrie, John Matarazzo, and the Charisma Media family: Thank you for bringing this book to life. Steve, your fifty-year legacy at Charisma is a testament to bold gospel work. You're a giant, and I'm honored to call you friend.

Adrienne Gaines: Your editing, especially during the hectic 2025 season, was exceptional. Thank you.

Patrick Conley: Your partnership turned this vision into a polished manuscript. You're an invaluable friend and ministry partner.

Gary West, Mike Forbis, and Dr. Malachi O'Brien: Your friendship, faithfulness to Christ, and inspiring lives make me a better man and leader. Thank you.

Helen: Your life and witness continue to shape Kelly and me, guiding how we engage the world. You are loved. You are family.

Bob Baker: My passion for sharing Jesus was sparked by you, a college student, taking me, a middle schooler, to find kids for church on Sundays. Though you're gone, your impact endures. I'm forever grateful.

To the Jesus Revolution Kids at Pathway Church, especially Dallas Davis and Junior Muhubao: Your bold witness, fervent prayers, and revival fire have transformed our city and church. Don't hold back—turn it up.

To our Cambodian People for Care & Learning family:

In a 98 percent Buddhist nation, your fearless proclamation of Christ is changing eternity. Your zeal, courage, and Holy Spirit power are reshaping Cambodia.

To the Buy a Tree. Change a Life. team across America: Your tireless work, radical generosity, and unity are advancing the gospel and forging a brighter future. Thank you.

ABOUT THE AUTHOR

Travis Johnson is the lead pastor of Pathway Church, a multisite church with global impact. His televised broadcasts inspire Christians to declare truth, transform lives, and change the world. His international work is focused on orphan care, education, church planting, peace initiatives, and economic development through his work as executive director of People for Care & Learning. He's also the founder of Buy a Tree. Change a Life., a member of the National Faith Advisory Board, and a former member of the Church of God executive council. He and his wife, Kelly, live in Mobile, Alabama, and have three kids: Kourtney, McKenna, and Blake. Find out more at pastortravisjohnson.com.